What people are

# Field of Blessings

Dr Ji Hyang Padma's brilliant book, *Field of Blessings: Buddhist Healing Through the Field of Consciousness*, pulls together the essential of Buddhist healing, rituals and practices in an accessible way for all to read. There is a wealth of information for those in the West who struggle to understand the various sects and practices of Buddhism while artfully relating it to the western mind and consciousness.

**Dr. Ann Drake**, author of *Healing of the Soul: Shamanism & Psyche*

In *Field of Blessings*, Ji Hyang Padma provides a remarkable exploration and comprehensive research into traditional Buddhist healing practices. Within Ji Hyang Padma's clear explanation she writes that although each Buddhist lineage has its own unique healing rituals we are working across lineages to identify the rituals that unite the practices. I found this book so engaging with seeds of truth about elements of healing that will enrich all who read this book.

*Field of Blessings* is a brilliant book that clears up so many misconceptions about Buddhist healing rituals. And what a better guide than Ji Hyang Padma who is a gifted Buddhist teacher, counsellor and healer. Throughout the book she illustrates how Buddhist healing practices reconnect clients to the ground of being and deepens their connection with the natural world. I was so impressed how Ji Hyang Padma's knowledge clearly shines through as well as her deep love and commitment to the work.

**Sandra Ingerman**, award winning author of 12 books on shamanism including *Soul Retrieval*

Ji Hyang Padma's *Field of Blessings* shows us traditional and modern Buddhist approaches to the mystery that the whole world is medicine. And, with that, invites us into exploring the actual realities of a holistic vision of healing both body and mind. This is an important book for all of us on the paths of healing.
**James Ishmael Ford**, author of *Introduction to Zen Koans: Learning the Language of Dragons*

If Mindfulness is a haiku on the tip of the iceberg of Buddhist healing tradition, Ji Hyang's Field of Blessing reveals the stunning and awe inspiring depth of all that lies below.
**Brett Bevell**, author of *Energy Healing for Everyone, and Reiki for Spiritual Healing*

This is a book we have been waiting for. Ji Hyang Padma wrote a book which can be a major resource for awakening and healing for those who are on the spiritual path. Her research on Buddhist healing rituals is historically grounded and practically helpful. This is her big bodhisattva action for today's struggling people with many forms of traumas. I will use this book in my classes and recommend it highly for all people who are longing for recovering wholeness and well-being.
**Hyun Kyung Chung, Ph.D**. Professor of Interfaith Engagement, Union Theological Seminary

Ji Hyang Padma knows the words of Buddhism, she also knows the music, and she writes in a clear and engaging way. This is an important book because it gives readers a factually accurate exposition on historical Buddhism, while also recognizing the practices and rituals of Buddhism are an empirically developed neurophysiology on altered consciousness.
**Stephan A. Schwartz**, author of *The 8 Laws of Change*

Going beyond familiar mindfulness practices to introduce readers to the vast repertoire of healing rituals found in traditional Buddhism Ji Hyang Padma's new book is aptly named. It will be a blessing not only for students and scholars but for individuals and healers across traditions as well as in my context as part of a multi-faith university chaplaincy. I appreciate having such a carefully researched, accessibly written guide not only for understanding but for applying Buddhist practices in a world hungry for wholeness and healing.

**Dr. Jennifer Howe Peace**, Tufts University Chaplain

*Field of Blessings*: what a beautiful and fitting title for this book that examines the role of the field of consciousness in healing, with a particular focus on Buddhist Healing. Dr Ji Hyang Padma explains that when the absolute and universal nature of consciousness, Dharmakaya, the "substrate out of which all animate and inanimate forms arise", is understood and consciously engaged with, then wholeness and true healing is found in every situation. This approach to healing knows implicitly that every human being is deeply related to every other human being, indeed, to all of life itself. In this setting, in addition to receiving the intended healing, the human being is also blessed with the realization that they are not only a part of the healing process but also part of the broader creation itself. This is the foundation of healing and spiritual well being.

**Paul Mills**, Professor of Family Medicine and Public Health Chief, Division of Behavioral Medicine Director

# Field of Blessings

Ritual & Consciousness in the Work
of Buddhist Healers

# Field of Blessings

## Ritual & Consciousness in the Work of Buddhist Healers

Ji Hyang Padma

MANTRA
BOOKS

Winchester, UK
Washington, USA

## JOHN HUNT PUBLISHING

First published by Mantra Books, 2020
Mantra Books is an imprint of John Hunt Publishing Ltd., No. 3 East Street, Alresford
Hampshire SO24 9EE, UK
office@jhpbooks.com
www.johnhuntpublishing.com
www.mantra-books.net

For distributor details and how to order please visit the 'Ordering' section on our website.

ISBN: 978 1 78535 644 5
978 1 78535 645 2 (ebook)
Library of Congress Control Number: 2017951919

A CIP catalogue record for this book is available from the British Library.

Design: Stuart Davies

UK: Printed and bound by CPI Group (UK) Ltd, Croydon, CR0 4YY
US: Printed and bound by Thomson-Shore, 7300 West Joy Road, Dexter, MI 48130

We operate a distinctive and ethical publishing philosophy in
all areas of our business, from our global network of authors to
production and worldwide distribution.

# Contents

To Ani Tendol and the nuns of **Keydong Thukche Choling** nunnery, for their practice.

# Part I

# Buddhist Healing

# Chapter 1

# Introduction

We are hungry for a direct experience of the sacred in Western culture. We try to fill the void with technology, and its "quick fix" of images and information. We uplift and idealize the newest smartphone release, revering the complexity of technology and the ingenuity of its creators.

However, this leaves us hungry for true connectivity. We don't need more complexity; we need greater depth. We don't need more information; we need more appreciation—the heartfelt expression of value and interconnection through gratitude provides a sense of meaning. That sense of meaningfulness is a gateway to the sacred, and a tremendous source of resiliency.

As the historian Mircea Eliade noted, human beings are "Homo symbolicus": we are naturally designed and driven to make meaning of our lives through the symbols of narrative. Narratives mediate between the inner world and the outer world, giving shape to our experience. Narratives can be spoken, written, or embodied. Ritual is performed narrative, embodied narrative. The rituals of traditional Buddhist medicine are powerful vehicles for spiritual transformation that reconnect clients with an embodied wholeness. The client's experience of his or her wholeness catalyzes healing on many levels.

Within contemporary culture, there is a degree to which the power of Buddhist healing arts is recognized. We have essentially borrowed MBSR (Mindfulness-Based Stress Reduction) from Buddhist tradition, and this has led to myriad mindfulness-based therapies. Certainly, the practice of mindfulness can restore a sense of health and wellbeing. However, in the adaptation of mindfulness to the culture of conventional medicine, the particular nuances and skillful means found in traditional healing have been lost in translation. The incorporation of mindfulness into contemporary healing arts is a good beginning, but not quite as comprehensive as the healing rituals found within the vast repertoire of traditional Buddhism.

I was inspired to conduct this research into traditional healing practices by my own deep commitment to working as a Buddhist teacher, counselor, and healer. As a mindfulness teacher, I have been well aware that traditional Buddhist practices draw from a deeper well—one which includes, but is not limited to, mindfulness.

Chod, Medicine Buddha practices, and other traditional Tibetan rituals are used by healers to evoke sacred energies. These rituals create the ground for experiences of radical empathy between client and healer, support psychospiritual integration of the healing crisis, and also contact deep archetypal realms of the psyche. In reclaiming the power of ritual within healing, we have access to a deeper well than object-materialism provides.

While some modernists take an ahistorical approach to mindfulness, considering all other practices to be cultural detritus, it is evident that the practices of Buddhist meditation and traditional Buddhist healing practices evolved across the centuries together. In the traditional context, Tibetan doctors included a spectrum of modalities in their practice: counseling, hands-on work, subtle-energy medicine, ceremonies, and meditation teaching. We could then consider these practices in their totality the earliest psychology.

What I have found through my own journey with these healers is that traditional healing rituals help reconnect clients with their relationship to the ground of being, to their relationships and the natural world. This shift in consciousness supports physical healing. As one healer noted, "First the consciousness changed, and then the body changed." Understanding the role of consciousness in healing could be key to the development of subtle-energy modalities for use in the helping professions that work with the client's body, mind, and energy.

The future of psychology is now well positioned to validate its past. The efficacy of traditional subtle-energy healing can now be measured by state-of-the-art subtle-energy research, as evidenced by Chevalier (2012), Hammerschlag et al. (2014), and many others. Cutting-edge research in consciousness studies shows that meditation supports the development of nonlocal consciousness, while ritual serves as a protocol, which focuses the healing intention of nonlocal consciousness, and strengthens it (Schwartz, 2018). Through the incorporation of archetypal work and subtle-energy healing practices, contemporary psychology may transcend its self-imposed limits, towards the achievement of a truly transpersonal psychology.

It is my intention to actually strengthen our societal capacity for healing by bringing forward the wisdom and practices of Buddhist healing lineages in a way that is accessible to the uninitiated, so that we can together recover a sense of the sacred in everyday life, and develop a richer, deeper culture of healing within contemporary society.

May the great work begin.

# Chapter 2

# Buddhist Healing — A History

In understanding Buddhist approaches to healing it is essential to visit these practices within the context of their deep historical and cultural background. We will begin by visiting the teachings of the historical Buddha, and dive into the core teaching of *paticca samupadda*, the Buddhist doctrine of interdependent origination, which prepared the ground for the diverse healing paths in practice today. We will follow the development of *paticca samupadda* through Mahayana Buddhist teachings. We will then trace the applications of this relational worldview as it concerns Buddhist healing praxis.

Certain studies of Buddhist healing have focused on the ultimate goal of liberation, to which other goals are subsumed (Mumford, 1989; Sumegi, 2008). They have suggested that the Buddhist focus on enlightenment does not afford space or time to the resolution of such practical concerns as physical health. However, this does not fully take into account the vast and subtle implications of *paticca samupadda*, which describes the interdependence of consciousness and the physical world.

A more nuanced understanding of the function of *paticca samupadda* with reference to Buddhist understandings of healing can be achieved through the concomitant use of the Mahayana doctrine of *trikaya*, commonly referred to as the three bodies of Buddha. The *trikaya* describes three bodies, or orders, of reality, which are interdependent and inseparable from each other: the ultimate order of reality; the relative order of reality; and the subtle-energetic order, the subtle body. Some Buddhist approaches to healing focus upon the literal physical body, some teachings focus upon the ultimate wholeness of our life experience, and some work with the subtle-energy body to bring

7

about healing. These different aspects of healing work can be seen, like the *trikaya*, as interdependent, and ultimately a unified whole.

## Early Historical References

Within the cultural context of ancient Buddhism, healing was understood to be a somato-emotional integrative process that restores wholeness to both individuals and communities. The process of achieving integration is found within the Middle Way between indulgence and self-mortification (Armstrong, 2004); in this regard, healing practices were a natural adjunct to meditation (Tatz, 1985). That understanding of healing was woven into the early sutras (teachings of the Buddha) through the core teaching of *paticca samupadda*, the law of interdependent origination—or, as it is often known, the law of cause-and-effect. We are now going to track that understanding of healing as it unfolded across time and cultures.

## Paticca Samupadda: Interdependence

The vision of interdependent origination, *paticca samupadda*, that has been articulated in early Buddhist texts and progressively developed through generations of teaching, places the individual Buddhist practitioner's process of integration within a context of radical inclusiveness.

To understand the broad implications of this way of seeing things in connection to each other—a view which is absolutely central to our explorations—it is essential to begin with an examination of the teaching of dependent origination in its original textual context. Joanna Macy (1978) has provided a valuable English rendering of the Pali term, *paticca samupadda*:

> Uppada, the substantive form of the verb uppajjati, means "arising"; sam-uppada, "arising together." Paticca, as the gerund of paccati (pati + I, to "come back to" or "fall back

on"), is used to denote "grounded on" or "on account of."
Literally, then, the compound would mean "on account of
arising together" or, since it is used as a substantive, "the
being-on-account-of-arising-together." (p. 16)

This teaching is associated with Buddha's original insight, at the
moment of Enlightenment. At that moment, this is the Buddha's
core realization, the breakthrough: Each element of existence is
conditioned by other elements. Perception itself arises through a
convergence of factors; it depends upon that which is perceived.
Consciousness and name-and-form rest upon each other like
"two sheaves of reeds leaning on each other" (Bodhi, 2000, p.
607). *Paticca samupadda* is also referred to as mutual causality,
interdependent origination, dependent origination, and mutual
arising: Within Buddhist studies, these terms are considered
roughly synonymous with each other. This teaching is often
described within the Pali Canon with a four-line verse:

*When this is existing, that comes to be;*
*with the arising of this, that arises;*
*when this does not exist, that does not exist;*
*with the ceasing of this, that ceases.*
(Maha Ghosananda, 1991, p. 20)

This teaching expresses a causal paradigm that is profoundly
relational. Macy (1978) has described this insight succinctly:
"The subject of thought and action (self) is in actuality a
dynamic pattern of activity in interaction with its environment
and inseparable from existence" (p. 112). When the self is
recognized as fluid, and arising interdependently with other
beings, this heals the illusion of separation that is at the root of
*tanha* (craving) and *dukkha* (suffering). From this perspective, the
Buddha is, in early texts, sometimes called the Great Physician:
He restores wellbeing through reconnecting his patients with

self-insight. This has profound implications for the way that we, as individuals, live and move, and have our being. If we are not separate from others, there is nothing to protect or defend. Another person's happiness is also our happiness. Through our connection to all of life, we flourish together.

In the *Lotus of the Good Law Sutra*, a parable is used to describe the practice of meditation. Within this story, Buddha identified desire, anger, and ignorance as the causes of illness, like "wind, bile, phlegm," the ancient medical classifications of the core physical vectors of illness (Clifford, 2006, p. 23). The medicinal plants used to heal these illnesses are the Four Noble Truths. Through awareness that there is no separate self, these afflictive thought-patterns are seen as empty, and lose their power to afflict the individual.

In addition to the liberating effect of *paticca samupadda* upon the ego's pattern of crystallizing and reifying the self, the law of dependent origination has several more implications. First, this teaching demonstrates the interdependence of the knower and the known (Macy, 1978). Within the teaching of dependent origination, each perception that we give rise to can be seen as coming into being through our interaction with the perceived. In order to see, there must be an eye, visual consciousness, and an object of sight; to hear a sound is dependent upon the ear, auditory consciousness, and the sound being heard—and so it is with all the senses, including the sixth sense enumerated, thought (Bodhi, 2000). Therefore, there is no ultimate formulation of truth: Knowing is always conditioned by the relationship of the knower and the known. Contemporary scientists who study consciousness are re-discovering this insight. Quantum physics has shown that the knower and the known are energetically connected: By observing the world, we already influence it. We will address these scientific implications in greater depth in a later chapter. In the final analysis, this is ultimately good news.

It is the illusion that the knower is separate from and unconditioned by the world he would know that drives him into error. (Macy, 1978, p. 131)

When the dependent co-arising nature of his mental processes is acknowledged then his knowing enhances his conscious connection with and participation in the reality surrounding him...there is no knower or known so much as "just knowing." (Macy, 1978, p. 142)

The law of *paticca samupadda* also lifts the nature of the relationship of mind and body into the light of interdependence. In the *Nidanavagga Sutta*, which describes this teaching in depth, consciousness and name-and-form (the physical) are compared to "two sheaves of reeds, resting upon each other" (Bodhi, 2000, p. 602).

I should mention, as well, that the early discourses of the Buddha also contain many graphic descriptions of the body's transient nature, which are less poetic. There is a clear purpose for these descriptions. They parallel the suttas' descriptions of the composite, changeable nature of mind—illustrating that ultimately nothing remains, nor is, one (Macy, 1978). In my own experience, working as an EMT (emergency medical technician), an awareness of the body's impermanence was an excellent catalyst to look deeper, beyond the physical body to the core of being. At the same time, the relationship between the body and mind is honored by this image of the reeds that lean upon each other; consciousness and the physical body are in a dance. When we are having an emotional or physical experience, sometimes the physical body leads, sometimes the mind precipitates the physical sensation. We will go into this dance further, within Chapter 13, when we discuss interpersonal neurology.

This image of consciousness and physical form coming-into-being together indicates a deep respect for the physical world—a respect that is underscored by the story of the Buddha's

Enlightenment: At the moment when Buddha was assailed by the forces of doubt, he touched the Earth. As the historian Karen Armstrong (2004) has noted:

> The earth-witnessing posture...makes the profound point that a Buddha does indeed belong in this world. ...The Dhamma is exacting, but it is not against nature. There is a deep affinity between the Earth and the selfless human being. ...The man or woman who seeks Enlightenment is in tune with the fundamental structure of the Universe. (p. 92)

The interdependent connection between *nama rupa* and consciousness also carries deep-reaching ethical implications. If we are deeply related, in fact inextricably connected at our core to the world around us, it follows that a person with insight will treat the body, the physical world, and all his or her relationships with care and reverence. The *Digha Nikaya Sutta* described the connection in this way:

> Just, Vasettha, as a mighty trumpeter makes himself heard — and that without difficulty — in all four directions; even so of all things that have form or life, there is not one that he passes by or leaves aside; he respects them all with mind set free and filled with deep-felt love (D II. 443). (Carpenter & Rhys Davids, 1977, p. 147)

Implicit within this interdependence is both love and responsibility. In the light of *paticca samupadda*, the self is an interdependent and emergent relational process, mutually created by and creating the society around it. This is reflected in the elevation of Sangha (community) within Buddhist teaching, and in fact all the social teachings within Buddhism (Macy, 1978). In this light, compassion is not an intended action; it is a natural action: the recognition that we are both part of a greater whole that is the web of life, and the world around us.

While there are many direct references to *paticca samupadda* in the Pali Canon, this core teaching really is suffused throughout the early Buddhist teachings of the Pali Canon and also throughout later teachings. The way to understand this teaching on mutual causality that reaches everywhere and yet is considered "deep and subtle" (Macy, 1978, p. 53), not easily grasped, is described in the Pali Canon with the phrase *yoniso manasikara*.

> Manasikara is from a verb meaning "to ponder," to "take to heart," and denotes deep attention or attentive pondering. Here this pondering is qualified by yoniso, the ablative of yoni. Yoni, literally, is "womb." By extension it came to mean "origin," "way of being born" and "matrix." The connotations of this compound with regard to paticca samupadda are multiple. On the one hand it connotes generation, the arising of phenomena, and on the other, as "matrix" it suggests the web of interdependence in which these phenomena participate. Such thinking, then…is not a dissecting or categorizing exercise of the intellect. Synthetic rather than analytic, it involves an awareness of wholeness—an intent openness or attentiveness wherein all factors can be included, their relationships beheld. (Macy, 1978, p. 53)

So, as fellow explorers, we can pause for a moment to digest this teaching. The way to understand a relational universe is by seeing with eyes of wholeness: by connecting with our body, breathing deeply as we reflect on this. As we do so, we access the body's wholeness, and through this, we know our wholeness with all beings and the world. By doing so, we are entering into communion with the web of interdependence ourselves. This will prove key to the Buddhist healing practices explored in the pages that follow.

## Early Buddhist Healing Practices

As we take the next step, tracking Buddhist healing across the centuries, we can thankfully draw upon the studies of Buddhist healing that have gone before us. We know, for instance, that Buddhist monastic communities played an essential role in the development of Indian medicine. Because the healers made contact with all castes of people, they were considered ritually impure within Vedic rites, which meant that healing was problematic for upper-caste practitioners of Hinduism. However, the ancient medicine teachers found acceptance and willing students among the monks, who were instructed, within the Buddhist teachings, not to give heed to a person's caste. In fact, the entire practice of medicine fit well within the Buddhist teaching of the Middle Way—as students were counseled neither to reject the physical body, nor to attach to it, but to maintain its health and wellbeing for the purposes of meditation practice. This close association of Buddhist monks with the healing arts also supported the propagation of Dharma teaching in new countries. It was actually in the early centuries of the Common Era that the pharmacopeia and practices developed under the auspices of itinerant healers were assimilated back into Hinduism, whereupon they became known as Ayurvedic medicine (Zyzk, 1991).

On the basis of this deep awareness of interrelationship, a Buddhist ethics of care and concern was developed within the day-to-day life of the Sangha, the community of monks:

The person who returned first from town with the food donated by the village prepared the dining space, and heated the water for cooking. The one who arrived last from town completed the washing-up. "We are very different in body, Lord," one of the monks told the Buddha about his community. "But we have, I think, only one mind." (Armstrong, 2004, p. 141)

Many of these ethical teachings that ground *paticca samupadda* in everyday life are gathered within the Vinaya, a collection of guidelines for the monastic community. Several of these passages describe the healing care to be provided in times of illness. Within one traditional story, Shakyamuni Buddha went to visit a monastery where one monk was found in bed experiencing dysentery. Buddha asked the monk, "Does anyone tend you?" The monk replied, "They do not." At that time, the Buddha washed the monk himself, with Ananda's help, and made him as comfortable as possible. He then convened a meeting of the community, and reminded the other monks to look after each other, saying "Whoever tends the sick tends me" (Tatz, 1985, p. 32). This continuity of care, from the absolute cure of liberation through the earthy offering of hands and heart involved in tending dysentery, is all in the service of *paticca samupadda* and its web of relationships.

## Mahayana Developments: Emptiness and Skillful Means

Perhaps, in a sense, all Buddhist texts on healing can trace the roots of their teaching to *paticca samupadda*. However, there are particular differences in this expression of the dynamics of healing across the schools and vehicles of Buddhism. For instance, when health is used as a metaphor to describe freedom from the illness of self-clinging, early Buddhist texts (those composed from 334 BCE up to the Common Era) and Theravadan texts emphasize the medicine of renunciation, which brings freedom from desire. Mahayana Buddhist texts emphasize the medicine of *sunyata*, emptiness: seeing through the illusion of separateness in order to develop compassion, which cures the poison of anger, and the development of wisdom, which cures ignorance (Clifford, 2006). Due to the increasing misidentification of itinerant healers as ordained monks by laypeople (Zyzk, 1991), some early Theravadan texts prohibited monks and nuns from practicing the healing arts upon laypeople: There were concerns within the community that these practices caused monks to be seen as overinvolved in worldly pursuits (Tatz, 1985, pp. 36–9). However, medicine was always properly recognized as an essential element of Buddhist studies: Between the sixth and eleventh centuries CE, medicine was among the subjects monks studied at Nalanda University, the acclaimed Buddhist monastic seminary. With the advent of the Mahayana tradition, Buddhist texts took a much more liberal approach to the practice of medicine (Tatz, 1985).

The space for this cultural shift was cleared by the renowned Mahayana Buddhist philosopher Nagarjuna, who served as a teacher at Nalanda University (Ramanan, 1987). Through exceptionally insightful and creative interpretation of the early teachings of the Buddha, Nagarjuna developed the concept of *sunyata* (emptiness) as a way of describing the teaching of *paticca samupadda*. Nagarjuna expanded upon common understandings of *paticca samupadda* through his doctrine of *no-self*, an awareness that all phenomena are empty of an independently constituted self (Johnson, Robinson, & Bhikkhu, 2005). Although this matter may seem subtle to the casual observer, Nagarjuna's theory marks an important shift in Buddhist understandings of the nature of reality. It serves as a demarcation between the Mahayana school of Buddhism, which embraced this explanation, and the Theravadan school, those followers who considered this a departure from Buddha's historical teaching. In order to support his identification of *paticca samupadda* (the mutual arising of phenomena) with *sunyata* (emptiness), Nagarjuna developed the doctrine of *upaya*, commonly known as skillful means. While the cultivation of nondual wisdom—the wisdom at the heart of emptiness and *paticca samupadda*—is the ultimate goal for all Buddhists, this practice is balanced by *upaya*, the skillful application of various means in service to others (Makransky, 2000).

Skillful means includes the infinite scope of activities and methods through which buddhas and bodhisattvas communicate Dharma (the Buddhist teaching) in the precise ways appropriate to the capacities of all living beings...the methods that buddhas and bodhisattvas employ to reach beings are as diverse as beings themselves, and are operative through all space and time. (Makransky, 2000, pp. 116–17)

Let's look again at our discussion of *paticca samupadda* a few pages ago, in which we noted that deep mutuality between consciousness and the body, that cosmic dance through which consciousness and the world are forever interconnected. The doctrine of *upaya* underscores, and reaffirms, that mutuality between consciousness and *nama rupa*. While Buddhism does emphasize ultimate liberation, the means for achieving that liberation include engagement with the world, and practices drawn from every element of the physical, immanent world. While Buddhist texts commonly lift up an ultimate healing that comes through seeing through the illusion of separation, this does not at all preclude healing work that is done on the relative level, to bring about physical health and mind-body integration.

The great teacher, Nagarjuna, who propounded the doctrines of *sunyata* and *upaya*, was also a master of Ayurvedic medicine. Within the Nagarjuna school of Ayurvedic medicine, the development of a pharmacopeia of mineral substances included the discovery of processes that rendered these minerals safe for human consumption. These therapeutic interventions continue to be an integral part of Ayurvedic medicine. Nagarjuna authored a pivotal commentary on the Ayurvedic text, *Susrata's Samhita*, and continued writing treatises on medicine as he developed the concept of interdependent origination through the *Prajna Paramita* sutras (Lad, 2002; Ninivaggi, 2008). Nagarjuna's life was a shining example of ultimate and relative healing pathways, practiced with equal ardor.

## Mahayana Healing Narratives

Nagarjuna's healing insight into emptiness served as a landmark for future generations of Buddhist scholars and practitioners. One of the most powerful developments of Nagarjuna's teaching on emptiness can be found in Tu-Shun's account of Indra's Net. Tu-Shun, founder of the influential Hua-Yen school of Chinese Buddhism in the seventh century, also served as a healer. Tu-Shun described emptiness, and the way all things come into being together, using the parable of Indra's Net. Envisioning a net, we can imagine jewels at every point where the threads of netting intersect. Each jewel is reflecting, not only every other jewel, but every reflection of every other jewel, so that all jewels are reflected in one. In this way, we can see that any one thing in the universe is inextricably tied together with the arisings of all other things, and interconnected with the entire universe (Cleary, 2000).

Another succinct description of the interwoven nature of personal and collective healing as described through *paticca samupadda* and *sunyata* is found in the *Hua-Yen Sutra*, which describes the "field of blessings" (Tsiknopoulos, 2019) that is generated by the awakened presence of the healer-teacher.

ཇི་ལྟར་ཆུ་ནི་རོ་གཅིག་གྱུང་། །སྣོད་ཀྱི་དབང་གིས་རྣམ་པར་འགྱུར། །དེ་བཞིན་སངས་རྒྱས་ཡོན་ཕུལ་བ། །རྒྱུད་ཀྱི་རྣམས་ལ་རྣམ་པར་འགྱུར།

*Just as water has but one taste,*
*Yet takes form through the power of its vessel;*
*Likewise too is the Buddha's field of blessing:*
*For it takes its form for each continuum of mind.*

ཇི་ལྟར་མཁས་པའི་རྒྱལ་པོ་དག། །འགྲོ་བ་མང་པོ་ཤེས་པར་བྱེད། །དེ་བཞིན་སངས་རྒྱས་ཡོན་ཕུལ་བ། །ཇི་ལྟར་བསྐྱེད་བཞིན་ཤེས་པར་བྱེད།

*Just as wise kings,*
*Serve to understand many living beings;*
*Likewise too is the Buddha's field of blessing:*

*(ji ltar bkyed bzhin shes par byed).*
For it acts to understand things when they arise, just as they are.

།དེ་ལྟར་དྲི་མེད་མེ་ལོང་ལ། །ཅི་འདྲའི་གཟུགས་རྣམས་དེ་བཞིན་སྣང་། །དེ་བཞིན་སེམས་ཅན་བསམ་ཚུལ་དུ། །སངས་རྒྱས་ཡོན་ ཏན་རྣམ་དག་འགྱུར།

Just as in a stainless mirror,
Any sort of forms appear just as they are;
Likewise too, according to sentient beings' ways of thinking:
The Buddha's field of blessing manifests as utterly pure.

།དེ་ལྟར་དུག་ཐབ་སྨན་གྱི་རྣམས། །དུག་ནད་ཐམས་ཅད་སོས་པར་བྱེད། །དེ་བཞིན་སངས་རྒྱས་ཡོན་ཐུལ་བ། །ཉོན་མོངས་དུག་ ནི་ཆེན་པོ་སེལ།

Just as medicines which cure poison,
Serve to heal all ailments of poisoning;
Likewise too is the Buddha's field of blessing:
For it dispels all ailments.

།དེ་ལྟར་ཉི་མ་ཤར་བ་ནི། །འགྲོ་བ་འདི་དག་སྣང་བར་བྱེད། །མུན་པ་དག་ཀྱང་རྣམ་པར་སེལ། །སངས་རྒྱས་ཡོན་ཐུལ་དེ་བཞིན་ ནོ།

Just as the shining sun,
Serves to illuminate all living beings;
Yet also dispels all darkness in full:
So too is the Buddha's field of blessing similar to that.

།དེ་ལྟར་ཟླ་བ་དྲི་མེད་པ། །ཀུན་ཏུ་མཉམ་པ་ཉིད་བྱས་ཏེ། །ས་ནི་རབ་ཏུ་སྣང་བར་བྱེད། །སངས་རྒྱས་ཡོན་ཐུལ་དེ་བཞིན་ནོ།

Just as the moon, free from clouds,
Shines upon all equally;
And thereby vigorously brightens the earth:
So too is the Buddha's field of blessing similar to that.

།དེ་ལྟར་ཆུ་ཡི་སྟོབས་དྲགས་ཀྱིས། །ས་རི་ཐམས་ཅད་གཡོ་འགྱུར་བ། །སངས་རྒྱས་ཡོན་ཐུལ་དེ་བཞིན་དུ། །བྱེད་གསུམ་འཚོར་བ་ རྣམས་ཀྱང་སྐྱོང་།

Just as, through the strong force of water,
All lands and mountains come to shake;

*Likewise too is the Buddha's field of blessing:*
*For it protects all those wandering in the three planes of existence.*

།འབར་དང་འོད་འཕྲོ་བཅས་པའི་མེ། །ཐམས་ཅད་དག་ཏུ་སྲེག་པའི་དངོས། །དེ་བཞིན་སངས་རྒྱས་ཡོན་ཕུལ་བ། །འདུ་བྱེད་ ཐམས་ཅད་སྲེག་པར་བྱེད།
*Just as fire, with blazing and radiant light,*
*Is the substance which incinerates all;*
*Likewise too is the Buddha's field of blessing:*
*For it incinerates all conditioned states.*

The *Hua-Yen Sutra* described the power of luminous awareness to heal and benefit all beings simply by reflecting back their innate clarity and wholeness. Everything already contains the entire universe: The Sage simply reflects this back to those he or she encounters. This understanding of healing as restoring an innate wholeness has its parallel in Wilhelm's classic story of the rainmaker.

In a Chinese village struck by drought, there was no recourse but to send for the rainmaker. Wilhelm, author of the Bollingen edition of *I Ching*, saw the old man arrive, and promptly request a secluded hut outside of the village. On the third day of his retreat there was a great downpour. Wilhelm asked about this: "So you can make rain?" The rainmaker replied that he could not. Wilhelm retorted, "Yet, there was immense drought when you arrived, and then, in three days, rain."

The old man replied, "That is different. I come from a region where people are in balance, and the rain is also in balance. People in this region had come out of alignment with the Tao, and with themselves. When I arrived here, I too succumbed to that imbalance, but when I was alone, came back into the Tao, and so naturally it rained" (Hannah, 1991).

The rainmaker, like Tu-Shun, is able to connect with his own wholeness—and through this awakened connection to the "jewel net" of interdependence, the gift of wholeness radiates out through the village, restoring the flow of nature. While the rainmaker is evidently Taoist, Taoism and Buddhism had been evolving in dialogue in that culture over many centuries. Wilhelm's story well describes a Mahayana Buddhist understanding of healing: Since we are always coming-into-being interdependently, the work each person does to awaken to his or her innate wholeness anchors that experience of healing for others—just as one jewel contains all others within Indra's Net.

As Mahayana Buddhist tradition continued to develop in the centuries that followed Nagarjuna, the doctrine of *upaya*, skillful means, provided its teachers with a certain flexibility: Buddhism was free to take the shape of the culture it found itself in, to employ teaching styles that were well suited to the pantheistic cultures of South and East Asia. Archetypal images of Bodhisattvas were developed to lift up different aspects of compassion and awakened insight. The Medicine Buddha, also known as Baisajyaguru (Sanskrit), Sangay Menla (Tibetan), and Yaksa Yorae Bul (Korean), became one of the most venerated Bodhisattvas.

Medicine Buddha practice, which was already established in the fourth century (Birnbaum, 1979; Thanh, 2001), continues through the present day. Through the ritual practices of the Medicine Buddha, which include chanting the *Medicine Buddha Sutra* and reciting the associated *mantra* (a phrase that is repeated as a meditative practice to bring the mind to a state of concentration, and may additionally have specialized uses— in this case, to bring healing) and visualizations, both the existential sickness of separation from innate wholeness and the relative sicknesses of the body and mind are considered to be cured (Birnbaum, 1979). Within the descriptions of the vows of the Medicine Buddha, physical healing is described in tandem with spiritual awakening. Within its stories of the deepest physical cures—for instance, a person brought back from coma—the spiritual healing is underscored by the client's return to consciousness with new insight into the patterns of interdependent origination within their life: They are completely transformed (Birnbaum, 1979).

From a neuropsychological perspective, it has been shown that chanting meditation has an integrative effect upon the nervous system: Melody links separated areas within the cortex, while rhythm connects the limbic system and prefrontal cortex areas of the brain, renewing an innate sense of wholeness (Siegel, 2010, p. 107). This is one of many findings in current research that confirm the healing properties of these meditation practices developed as skillful means.

At first glance, mantra and other practices developed specifically to support healing may appear goal-oriented and firmly stuck in a literal view of reality. However, many Buddhist teachers have confirmed that these apparently dualistic practices are skillful paths for harnessing mental energy in the service of awakening. The actual practice of reciting the mantra thousands of times can bring the mind to a place of stillness—in which it rests in the present moment. Through that direct experience of emptiness, a natural awareness of interdependence is renewed and an existential (and physical) healing may take place.

## Mahayana Healing Practices and the Perceptual States of the Trikaya: Ultimate and Relative Healing

Through examples such as this, we can see that Buddhist healing practices utilize *upaya* that work at different levels of truth in order to bring about wholeness. There is actually a paradigm within Mahayana Buddhism which provides a reference point. In early Mahayana Sutras, beginning with the fourth-century sage Asanga, the different levels of truth are described as the *trikaya* (three bodies, or three worlds): *Dharmakaya, Nirmanakaya,* and *Sambhogakaya* (Tatz, 1985). In early teachings the three kayas referred to the three bodies of the Buddha—the physical body, the Dharma (truth) body, and the subtle body. In Mahayana Sutras the three kayas/bodies are understood to be three mutually reciprocal realms, which together form a whole expression of consciousness and a complete understanding of existence (Schuhmacher & Woerner, 1991). In this vein, the three kayas can be translated as the realm of absolute truth, the realm of form, and the subtle realm or the realm of becoming. *Dharmakaya* represents the primordial body, Buddha nature itself: a "substrate out of which all animate and inanimate forms arise" (Schuhmacher & Woerner, 1991, p. 230). Sogyal Rinpoche (1992) has compared the Dharmakaya to David Bohm's implicate order, that dimension of Truth and energy which serves as the matrix of all tangible forms. *Nirmanakaya* represents the tangible, relative level: the world of *nama rupa*, name and form. *Sambhogakaya* is subtle energy: the dream body, which may be analogous to Bohm's super-implicate order, mediating between these two so that the energetic information of the Dharmakaya is conveyed to the Nirmanakaya (Schuhmacher & Woerner, 1991). These three levels of reality are interdependent with each other and are actually a unified whole. Going forward, we will reference these three realms, or levels of truth, in order to categorize Buddhist orientations towards healing.

## Dharmakaya: Ultimate Healing

The practice of healing by working on the ultimate level, for the goal of spiritual liberation, is the natural expression of Dharmakaya. Many Mahayana texts within Zen and Tibetan lineages have referenced the need to move beyond the duality of sickness and health, to see a healing wholeness in phenomena just-as-they-are, a sacred world hidden within the details of ordinary life. This view is most completely realized within the pivotal Mahayana text, the *Vimalakirti Sutra*, in which the highly realized lay teacher, Vimalakirti, manifests sickness in order to teach people not to cling to the physical body. The Buddha and his disciples then go to visit Vimalakirti, and inquire about his illness. Manjusri, who is considered the embodiment of wisdom, asks Vimalakirti:

"Householder, whence came this sickness of yours? How long have you had it? How does it stand? How can it be alleviated?" Vimalakirti replied, "Manjusri, my sickness comes from ignorance and thirst for existence and it will last as long as do all the sicknesses of all living beings. The bodhisattva loves all beings as if each were his only child. He becomes sick when they are sick and cured when they are cured. You ask me, Manjusri, whence comes my sickness; the sickness of the bodhissatva arises from great compassion." (Thurman, 1991, p. 43)

Vimalakirti describes what, from the Buddhist standpoint, can be considered the primary human ailment: We forget that we are already complete, already pure consciousness. The Bodhisattva re-enters this realm of duality out of great love, and stays within *Maya*, the play of illusion that is human existence, until all beings are healed. It is certainly true within all Buddhist lineages, even those that contain specific healing arts, that their ultimate fulfillment is not found within relative cures for physical suffering. It rests upon the ultimate healing that Vimalakirti describes: resting the mind in its innate clarity, regardless of situation.

There is a contemporary story that illustrates this point. When Tibetan teacher Tulku Urygen Rinpoche was having a heart attack, his students asked him why he was sick; surely meditation could cure his heart. Tulku Urygen replied that there are in fact yogic practices that can have a strong impact on health and longevity, but you have to work at them pretty hard and in the end your body dies anyway. So he felt he would rather use his time to develop stability of mind (Chozen-Bays, Levy,

Rhodes, & Shlim, 2005, p. 38).

This story well exemplifies the Vajrayana, or "diamond vehicle"; Vajrayana is a meditation path generally understood to be within the Mahayana Buddhist tradition, with a focus on the relationship between consciousness and the material through a "unified body-mind field" (Samuel, 2014, p. 33). The Vajrayana view of seeing all phenomena as inseparable from luminous emptiness is exemplified by this poem, "It's All Basically Good."

*Illness and its painfulness have neither base nor root.*
*Relax into it, fresh and uncontrived.*
*Revealing dharmakaya way beyond all speech and thought.*
*Don't shun them, pain and illness are basically good.*

*What confusion takes to be taking place is negative force's work*
*But it's all your own mind, simple, unborn, unceasing.*
*Without anxiety or even worrying at all,*
*Don't shun them: demons and gods are basically good.*

*When the agony of illness strikes your fourfold elements,*
*Don't grasp at its stopping; don't get angry when it won't improve.*
*Such adversities have the flavor of bliss that's free of contagion's blight.*
*These kleshas are not to be shunned; they are basically good. ...*

*And though this whole life is plagued by the torments of falling ill*
*Don't think that's bad; don't plan to get around it.*
*Then it will be your badge, your proof of conduct of equal taste.*
*Your suffering is not to be shunned; it's basically good.*
(Gotsangpa, 2012, p. 245)

Gotsangpa's poem illustrates the core insight of the Dharmakaya approach: Spiritual growth sometimes becomes more real when practice is more difficult. In particular, it can be deepened by working with the raw energies of illness, bringing awareness to the experience of pain. Through this a practitioner attains the realization of "equal taste": discovering within the phenomena of illness the play of emptiness that is the nature of mind. This truly is an advanced realization of the practice of *paticca samupadda*.

However, with an elementary skill level, mindfulness meditation can be seen to shift pain thresholds. Zen Master Jan Chozen-Bays has described the way she has seen this with her students:

> When the mind is very quiet, time seems to stretch and things are moving very slowly, so the moment of sensation and the discomfort are separated by empty space. Each one is experienced discretely. As a result, the usual experience of pain is not there. The sensation of pain comes from connecting all those moments. When they are not connected, when the mind is open and spacious and experiences are separate, it isn't pain anymore. (Chozen-Bays, Levy, Rhodes, & Shlim, 2005, p. 40)

Gotsangpa (2018) and Chozen-Bays' accounts agree at this point: When a person is able to rest within the immediacy of moment-to-moment experience, the pain that arises is not accompanied by anxiety or other mental turbulence; within pain, there need not be suffering. Through mindfulness, one makes contact with that moment-to-moment awareness that is pure perception, devoid of concept.

From a neurological perspective, mindfulness shifts the dominant mode of neural processing from a top-down flow associated with memory-based processing to the bottom-up flow of direct experience—which is spontaneous, always-emerging, *just this* (Siegel, 2010). So, it is evident that working with physical pain on the absolute level of Dharmakaya can have very tangible benefits with regard to the relative, Nirmanakaya level of reality.

## Nirmanakaya: Physical Healing

As we have seen, through a close look at *paticca samupadda*, that the realms of consciousness and the physical body are interdependent, it is evident that Buddhist healing practices directed upon ultimate and relative levels are also interdependent. Historically, these practices absolutely depended upon one another, as the transmission of these teachings took place across mountains and valleys, from one country to the next. The scholar Atisha, who conveyed essential Buddhist teachings from India across the Himalayas to Tibet in the eleventh century, also carried with him his work on Ayurvedic healing, *The Heart of Life*. To this day, Tibetan traditional medicine is strongly influenced by both Buddhist and Ayurvedic teaching lineages.

These sacred landscapes are also woven within the fabric of healing meditation practices, through the practices of the mandala, which represents both the microcosm, within an individual, and the macrocosm of a sacred universe. Within the mandala of the Medicine Buddha, the mandala's location is identified as Bodhgaya, where Shakyamuni Buddha attained Enlightenment. The seat of the Buddha, at the center of the mandala, is formed of lapis lazuli, the gem that is associated with healing and the Medicine Buddha. Rays of light emanate from the Buddha; he holds myrobalan, the great medicinal herb of the Himalayas, in his right hand. The Buddha is surrounded by a healing garden, by a retinue of protector Bodhisattvas and those who carry healing lineages, as well as four mountains that nurture the diverse range of medicinal herbs. Tibetan practitioners who are initiated into Medicine Buddha teachings visualize the mandala, and practice with it on three levels: on the outer level, paying homage to the Buddha and the healing arts; on an inner level, seeing oneself as the Medicine Buddha and all surroundings as the sacred circle of healing; on a secret level, seeing the Medicine Buddha as one's true nature, and the body as sacred healing space (Clifford, 2006). Since Tibetan meditative practice uses visualization and archetypal energies so creatively, there are naturally several auxiliary deities of healing that are associated with various psychospiritual qualities. The skillful methods (*upaya*) associated with the Medicine Buddha and other deities harness the imagination, and these interior landscapes, to bring about healing.

In the proactive use of visualization, Tibetan Buddhism can be seen to be very pragmatic. As Tulku Thondup notes:

> We all visualize constantly in daily life. Most of the time, our minds are occupied with neutral images or negative ones. If we develop the habit of seeing positive images instead, the peaceful nature of our minds begins to emerge and we give joy a chance to flourish. (Thondup,2013, pp. 34–5)

By transforming our mind, the resultant joy and clarity brings about healing on both physical and psychospiritual levels. There is now conclusive research that links chronic emotional distress with a rate of major disease that is twice that of the statistical norm (Thondup, 2013). Meditations that bring about clarity and inner peace can thus be seen to have a practical effect. This is in keeping with traditional Tibetan medicine, within which physical health is understood to correlate with a balanced mind and emotions. The heart and mind are considered synonymous within Tibetan medicine, and body/mind distinctions are ultimately seen as empty. This paradigm of seeing the body and mind as one is congruent with the roots of Tibetan medicine in Buddhism. Again, we can envision the mind and body in a continual dance with each other, wherein one leads and the other follows—or return to the classic image of consciousness and the physical form resting upon each other, like two sheaves of reeds. Within Tibetan medicine the root of illness is considered to be destructive emotional patterns. These reactive emotional habits condition compulsive behavior, which then predispose individuals to certain chronic imbalances of the mind and body (Dagpa & Dodson-Lavelle, 2009). Therefore, all treatment of physical illness within Tibetan medicine simultaneously works on treating the mind, so that the client can gain self-insight and break free from the grasp of the compulsive patterns that cause illness.

Through the meditations developed for healing, the body/mind arrives at a higher state of integration, which can then lead to higher realization. So, we can see that the literal, material Nirmanakaya realm and absolute Dharmakaya realm naturally exist in a state of reciprocity, an understanding that expresses the tenets of *paticca samupadda*.

### Sambhogakaya: Healing through the Subtle Body

We've charted the interdependence of the Nirmanakaya and Dharmakaya through traditional healing practices. Now, we will visit the third state that is pivotal in traditional Buddhist healing practices—the realm of Sambhogakaya, the place of the subtle body, dream states, and energetic activity that precede physical manifestation (Trungpa, 2003). The Sambhogakaya is harder to wrap our mind around, particularly in our materialist modern world that does not have anything that corresponds. To find modern parallels, we would need to look at movies such as *Cloud Atlas*, or ayahuasca journeys. And in fact, even advanced practitioners, and different practice lineages, interpret the Sambhogakaya in distinctly different ways. So we will proceed with care.

We have seen that the literal and absolute levels of truth are interdependent, through healing practices that affect both body and consciousness. Just in this way, the realm of the subtle body, the realm of physical reality, and the realm of awakened consciousness can be seen as interdependent. To get a more tangible sense of this ethereal terrain, we will visit the lucid dreaming and visionary practices utilized in South and East

Asian Buddhist cultures. These practices are, in many cases, closely related to the indigenous Nepali Gurung and Tibetan Bon visionary practices.

That connection with indigenous practices is no accident: Tibetan Buddhist culture has evolved in dialogue with local indigenous practices over many centuries. Mahayana Buddhism, due to the doctrine of *upaya*, skillful means, has the liberty to be syncretic, and take the shape of the cultural container it finds itself within.

Some scholars have asserted that shamanism and Buddhism differ with regard to their healing orientation; they have attributed a pragmatic "descending" focus to shamanism and an inner, "ascending" focus to Buddhism (Mumford, 1989; Wilber, 2000). From the scholarly perspective, it is tempting to treat shamanism and Buddhism as monoliths that can be neatly categorized. Yet, when we look at the great diversity within both shamanism and Buddhism, it is evident that such statements don't do justice to the spectrums of healing work and liberative sensibility found within each of these vast constellations of wisdom traditions. While there are places within Nepal where the Tibetan Buddhist and Nepalese shaman traditions have evolved side by side with a competitive edge (Mumford, 1989), there are also purely shamanic lineages within Tibetan Buddhist culture (Kressing, 2011; Sifers & Documentary Educational Resources, 2007). These shamanic lineages within Tibetan Buddhism are due to the fact that both the indigenous Tibetan Bon tradition and Tibetan Buddhism are syncretic in nature. Buddhism received unique gifts of power, ritual, and meaning-making from the dialogue with indigenous Bon practices, which began with Guru Rinpoche, the founder of Tibetan Buddhism.

From the very beginning, there has been some tension between these paths, as illustrated by the Buddhist story of the great sage Milarepa's competition with the Bon shaman Naro Bon Jung for dominion of Mount Kailash. Milarepa intended to strengthen the practice of Buddhism in Tibet, and in fact, he intended to re-establish its predominance as a spiritual practice. Therefore, Milarepa needed to prove its practical efficacy, and in so doing, create a place for it. So, he challenged Naro Bon Jung to a race: The first to summit Mount Kailash would receive the surrounding territory. Within this story, Milarepa's spiritual powers sped his ascension, and ensured his victory. From the perspective of Bon practitioners, there was never a quarrel between Milarepa and Bon practitioners, only peaceful coexistence; they attribute this story to later generations of Buddhist practitioners who were competitively-minded, and sought to suppress Bon.

Yet, over the centuries there has been bidirectional influence, and there are many shared values. Both of these traditions provide for the practical needs of their communities; both traditions lift up an ecological vision of interrelationship—through which individual relationships, brought into reciprocity, create a world in harmony (Abram, 1996; Macy, 1978; Snyder, 2000; Sumegi, 2008).

Many of the early Mahayana Sutras can be described as visionary journeys, akin to the shamanic practice of the vision quest. The early Mahayana *Pratyutpanna Samadhi Sutra* described the liberative power of working with visionary states. From the perspective of this Sutra, it is exactly these practices of working with visions and dreams that help us see the world and our concepts as not so solid, after all—and gain insight into *sunyata*, emptiness (Beyer, 1977). Buddhist healing traditions have, just as many shamanic lineages do, particular concepts of the subtle body and practices that use dreams and other nonordinary states of consciousness for purposes of transformation and healing.

We can make an important distinction between Buddhist practices and shamanic practices in their relation to these dream states. Within shamanic practices, dream encounters are more likely to be taken as real: This is dependent upon the individual shaman's meaning-making. Within Tibetan Buddhist practices, the yogi navigates this realm of Sambhogakaya in order to see all waking reality as illusion, all phenomena as empty of essential self (Sumegi, 2008). From a Buddhist perspective, it is through this knowledge that the dream-phenomena are empty of essential nature that one is able to intentionally navigate the dream worlds of subtle energy to bring about healing (Sumegi, 2008). Through practice navigating the dream worlds during life, the Buddhist practitioner would then be well prepared to navigate the *bardo*, or in-between realm after death, since that is also the realm of Sambhogakaya (Sumegi, 2008). All in all, within Tibetan Buddhist contexts, the practices of working with the subtle body, performing healings using visionary work, and guiding the deceased are seen as *upaya*, skillful means towards the ultimate attainment of *bodhicitta*, awakened heart-mind. In this, we see the interdependence of Dharmakaya, Sambhogakaya, and Nirmanakaya.

Given that Tibetan Buddhist lamas and indigenous practitioners alike practice divination, dreamwork, subtle-body healings, and death rites (Mumford, 1989), and that Bonpo practice and Tibetan Buddhist practice have been evolving in dialogue over many centuries, a bright line between Bon practice and Tibetan Buddhist practice is not easily drawn. While there is a historical record of competition, there are also certain points of convergence—most particularly, with regard to Chod ceremonies and practices related to the spirits of the land. As the Tibetan shaman Nyima put it, "There are many different elements in shamanism and Buddhist practice, but they are mixed together in the same bowl" (Peters, 2016, p. 67). It is thus not surprising that in recent years the 14th Dalai Lama recognized Bon as the "fifth tradition" within Tibetan spirituality (Berzin, 2000) on an equal footing with more orthodox Buddhist lineages (Kvaerne & Thargyal, 1993).

The scholar, David Abram, describes shamanic practice as a natural expression of the interdependence between human beings and the natural world. Viewed through this lens, the constellations of Buddhism and the constellations of shamanic practice come into close alignment. Within Tibetan Buddhist practice as expressed through Sambhogakaya, the perceptual state of subtle energy and dreamtime, *paticca samupadda* is described as *tendrel*, a direct experience of the all-pervasive nature of dependent origination, akin to the Western concept of synchronicity. Within this Tibetan understanding of interdependence, it is a given that the connections between cause and effect are not always visible to the casual observer. Sumegi (2008) has described the function of *tendrel* on the level of Sambhogakaya:

> In Buddhist theory, just as a particular experience is not constituted merely of a given set of external conditions but is also influenced by the subjective mind, so the omen or the tendrel becomes what it is through the mental attention and attitude of the experiencer. Crows cry in the trees all day, but when the mind pays attention to a particular event, and a particular feeling arises because of it, then one can speak of tendrel. ...Dudjom Rinpoche explains that the twelve links of dependent origination (tendrel) have both inner and outer manifestations. ...If [a person receiving a gift] recognizes it as a good omen, then by virtue of receiving it in that way he brings it into the "inner" tendrel (the twelvefold causation cycle) at the link of "feeling." (pp. 108–9)

So, we can understand the flow of energy and information initiated through work in the Sambhogakaya—dreams, nonordinary consciousness, and the subtle body—as part of a diagnostic continuum that includes physical, mental, and spiritual aspects of health (Sumegi, 2008). Within the framework of Tibetan medicine, the subtle body is carefully studied; and its treatment is an integral factor in healing. Just as the Sambhogakaya mediates between the spiritual realm of pure consciousness (Dharmakaya) and the physical realm (Nirmanakaya), the subtle body mediates between the extremely subtle body, described as the "indestructible drop" in the heart center, and the gross physical body through a system of channels, energy centers, and "winds."

> The mind is said to ride the "winds" as a rider rides a horse. The subtle winds flow throughout the channels, which in turn support the physical body and its physiological processes. ... Though no direct anatomical correlates exist, the subtle energy body can be seen as roughly corresponding to the Central Nervous System (CNS). A key point of correspondence is the high conductibility of the CNS—just as neurons transmit electrical signals which spark biochemical reactions throughout the nervous system, the mind "rides" the winds which pervade the channels and in turn effect change on the physical body. (Dagpa & Dodson-Lavelle, 2009, p. 183)

Through this integrative medicine paradigm, we can see the mutual causality of consciousness and the physical body expressed through the mediating principle of the Sambhogakaya, the subtle body. The physical body produces hormones and neurotransmitters in response to our initial assessment of a situation that affect the heart/mind, including the chemical catalysts of the fight-or-flight response. On the other hand, the inner freedom of the heart can pacify the emotional responses of the limbic system, and bring about a corresponding state of wellness within the physical body. In recognition of these causal links, Tibetan doctors prescribe yoga and meditation, as well as traditional herbal medicine, to bring about an optimum state of self-regulation.

Within Tibetan medicine, interdependence is recognized as a catalyst to healing, not only within the body-mind connection, but also within the physician-client relationship: The insight and compassion of the Tibetan physician is considered to have a direct effect on his ability to effect healing (Dagpa & Dodson-Lavelle, 2009). When herbal medicines and integrative practices are not effective, more invasive measures—such as acupuncture and moxibustion—are employed. These practices utilize the subtle body, opening blocks in its channels and restoring the flow of energy and information (Dagpa & Dodson-Lavelle, 2009). These somatic uses of the subtle body by Tibetan physicians overlap with the energetic uses of the subtle body by Tibetan shamans. The physician may treat a spiritual imbalance as a way of restoring mental and physical health; the shaman may access the subtle body and perform soul retrieval in order to cure a physical condition, such as repeated miscarriage. Because physical, spiritual, and mental health are seen as various manifestations of a core state of wellness, the specializations within Tibetan health are fluid, with physical proximity and personal relationships the primary factors in a client's choice of healing modality. In certain Tibetan refugee camps on the Tibet-Nepal border, the lhapas (shamanic practitioners) are the only health providers accessible to the Tibetan community (Sifers & Documentary Educational Resources, 2007).

Within rural Japan, traditional medicine also serves as an integrative bridge, drawing upon Buddhist paradigms of mutual causality in its expression of mind-body-spirit as an interdependent wholeness. The Japanese term for dependent origination is *engi*, which literally translates as "arising in relation" (Ehlers & Gethmann, 2010, p. 134). Japanese traditional medicine and Tibetan traditional medicine, in their maps of the subtle body and use of acupuncture and moxibustion to effect balance, draw from a shared heritage: traditional Chinese medicine, which migrated throughout Asia along the trade routes (Kaptchuk, 1999). Traditional healers in Japan have refined the art of moxibustion, which has evolved in folk culture in tandem with spirit mediumship and other uses of the Sambhogakaya (subtle body; Subramanian, 2002).

The dynamic relationship between moxa treatment, the dream body, and *engi* (mutual causality), is well described in Subramanian's interview of a traditional Japanese healer:

> Omuro, a 72 year old woman who heals terminally ill cancer patients, as well as people with less severe illnesses and disabilities, attests that her life keeps unfolding mysteriously, through oddly destined meetings with clients that appear in dreams or through sudden encounters. She states, "Once I dreamt of a woman admitted in a hospital. I didn't at first know why I was made to see such an image. But then I understood that I must meet and heal her illness. It was in the same town that my daughter resides in. And so I admitted myself in the hospital to get help on my knee that has withered from all the treatment I have done over the years—since I sit on the floor and fold my knees while healing. And in the hospital, after people had gone to sleep I would secretly work on this woman. Later, after I left the hospital since their help was ineffective, providing only temporary relief to my knee, I told the old woman to come to my place to get well.

On another occasion she recalls another patient with interest, a young Tabo in his early twenties, coming to her place for a brief visit with a distant acquaintance. She says:

> After his visit I could never stop thinking about him. He would appear in dreams and waking moments. At first I couldn't understand why. It was as if I was falling in love with him. Really! And as time went by, I knew he was suffering from cancer. He came here several years in a row and now is married and well. You know, when he was here, I would tell everyone of my young boyfriend and go on rides with him in

his car. (Subramanian, 2002, pp. 90–1)

Within Japanese traditional medicine, moxibustion is used with great precision to cure physical and mental imbalances. Moxa treatment uniquely supports the recovery of the mind-body-spirit continuum by penetrating many layers of the body/mind and inducing dreams (Subramanian, 2012). Through this restored connection with the wholeness of the client's experience, healing takes place simultaneously on the spiritual, energetic, and physical levels, illustrating the principle of mutual causality.

## Contemporary Approaches

We can see these ancient linkages between Buddhist teaching and physical healing translated into contemporary mind-body medicine through the work of Jon Kabat-Zinn, through his Mindfulness-Based Stress Reduction (MBSR) program. While Kabat-Zinn does not consider himself a Buddhist, he acknowledges the source of his own mindfulness practice as the Korean Zen and Vipassana Buddhist lineages. In this sense, we may consider his mindfulness-based stress reduction to be a secularized healing praxis with Buddhist roots. In Kabat-Zinn's mindfulness-based stress reduction protocol, the guiding principle is the restoration of the body-mind connection through mindfulness practice and yoga. The interdependence of consciousness and *nama rupa* (physical form) described by *paticca samupadda* is evident. Kabat-Zinn and others in the contemporary mindfulness movement also recognize those wider implications of this paradigm. Neuropsychologist Daniel Siegel describes the mind, brain, and relationships (with others and this world) as three prime facets of an open system that are continually influencing each other. As the individual comes into a greater state of wholeness and integration, the dynamic process of relational connection makes it possible for others to come into a state of integration, and see themselves as part of a whole. As David Bohm, the philosopher-physicist, writes, the words "medicine" and "meditation" are both rooted in the Latin *mederi*, which means "to cure." *Mederi* itself derives from an earlier Indo-European root meaning "to measure." Bohm notes that all things, then, possess their own "right inward measure" that makes them what they are. Meditation can be understood to be a way of taking measure, and realigning with a point of balance that is our right inward measure.

Bohm has an unparalleled capacity for making connections between cutting-edge science and integral spirituality, having mastered both fields. In this case, he sees the personal experience of wholeness experienced through mindfulness as a microcosm of a greater wholeness (Bohm, 2002, p. 177). In Bohm's understanding, this greater wholeness is described as the interplay between the unified whole (Dharmakaya) and the physical form (Nirmanakaya). So, this is tracking quite closely with the Buddhist model of the interdependence of mind and body, the individual and all his or her relationships. It also is a good fit for the three-faceted system Siegel describes: mind, brain, and relationships. There is a key difference between the traditional and contemporary models: The contemporary mindfulness models do not include the subtle body (Sambhogakaya), although they map its natural conduit, the nervous system, at great length (Kabat-Zinn, 1991; Siegel, 2010). The driving force within contemporary mindfulness has been to render these ancient teachings into secular language so that they can be reintegrated into the healing professions. Kabat-Zinn (2003) has seen the Buddha to be a natural "scientist and physician" (p. 145) who used his own mind and body as the basis for a phenomenological study, inquiring into the nature of our existence. Kabat-Zinn (2005) has well described the interdependence of personal mindfulness and societal wellbeing, conveying the essence of interdependence using examples drawn from medicine: While our dis-attention affects individual health and the state of our shared world, our attention and awareness also newly create the world.

Our state of mind and everything that flows from it affects the world. When our doing comes out of being, out of awareness, it is likely to be a wiser, freer, more creative and caring doing, a doing that can promote greater wisdom and compassion and healing in the world. The intentional engagement in mindfulness within various strata of society, and within the body politic, even in the tiniest of ways, has the potential, because we are all cells in the body of the world, to lead to a true flowering, a veritable renaissance of human creativity and potential, an expression of our profound health as a species and as a world. (Kabat-Zinn, 2005, p. 509)

Through the skillful adaptation of these ancient teachings on mindfulness to the context of modern secular society, thousands of people are finding relief from anxiety, depression, and other forms of suffering through the medicine of mindfulness. They may also glimpse the potential of a healing wholeness within our shared lives. In the emergence of these modern holistic paradigms of health and wellness, there is much to be celebrated. The work of reintegrating an understanding of the subtle body within the paradigms of integrative health is necessarily a task for the next generation.

## Conclusion

We can trace the development of practices of mindful attention, taught in tandem with the teaching of *paticca samupadda* (interdependent origination) towards the actualization of a state of healing wholeness, through the earliest discourses of the Buddha. This teaching of *paticca samupadda* describes a model of reality that is profoundly relational. The self is seen as a pattern of relationships, part of the continually interweaving matrix of life. Within this relational paradigm, body and consciousness are seen as specifically dependent upon each other. Taking a wider frame of vision, *paticca samupadda* describes the way that self and society arise together. The healing integration achieved by each individual radiates out, in widening circles, to the whole.

As the Mahayana schools of Buddhism came into being, new ways of understanding the mutual co-arising of individual and societal healing were developed, through the doctrines of *sunyata* and *upaya*, as well as through the rich and evocative images of the field of blessings, Indra's Net, and specialized devotional and meditative practices associated with the Medicine Buddha and healer Bodhisattvas. Within many Buddhist cultures, the connections between traditional medicine and Dharma are deeply interwoven. Buddhist approaches to healing can be classified by means of their perceptual focus within the three kayas, or bodies: Dharmakaya (absolute), Nirmanakaya (relative) and Sambhogakaya (intermediary, subtle energy). From the perspective of the Dharmakaya, the core insight of Buddhist practice is that wholeness can be found in every situation. However, the work at this ultimate level is interdependent with Buddhist healing practices that work to achieve integration at the somato-emotional level (Nirmanakaya), and practices that work with the subtle body (Sambhogakaya).

In the development of MBSR, Kabat-Zinn has translated these ancient teachings on wholeness into the modern languages of psychology and medicine—noting that paradoxically, it is through acceptance of the present moment and nonattachment to outcome that the healing wisdom of the mind/body is often activated (Kabat-Zinn, 2003). While Kabat-Zinn's pedagogical approach has not engaged the Sambhogakaya (subtle body) level of healing directly, his body scan and other mindfulness meditations thoroughly recalibrate the nervous system, and thus indirectly affect the healing of the subtle body. Through the power of presence, a healing attention naturally extends from our personal dimension of being, through all our relationships: Like the Jewel Net of Indra, it reaches everywhere. In this way, Kabat-Zinn's work is congruent with the adaptive and integrative approaches to healing that have been taken by Buddhist practitioners across millennia. The teaching of interdependence, across millennia, has provided many skillful means, which we will visit through the stories of traditional healers in the next few chapters. Within all these healing waters is one taste, the freedom of an essential wholeness that is present within each moment.

## Chapter 3

# Introduction to Buddhist Ritual

## The Need for Ritual

As we have noted in the Introduction, rituals are embodied narratives. We need these embodied narratives, because as humans we need story. We are designed and driven to make meaning of our lives through the symbols of narrative. The embodied narratives of healing ritual convey the meaning and intention created between the healer and client. They affect the flow of energy and information within the encounter, to bring about a change of consciousness and deep mind/body healing practice. As a prelude to our discussion of the specific rituals that healers used, let's first consider the Buddhist context of ritual.

## Buddhist Definitions of Ritual

There are several Tibetan words that convey the meaning of "ritual." *Choga* is the Tibetan translation of the Sanskrit *vidhi*, which means "manner or way of acting" or "rule": The term *choga* may refer to the guidelines for a ritual, or the ritual itself. The Tibetan definition of *choga* is "a method for accomplishing a goal." Within this broad understanding, we can consider all the healing practices described by these traditional healers as ritual. Ultimately, we are well served by letting the healers provide our final definition of ritual. It will arise from the healers' stories, and from the healers' own understandings of their work.

## Cultural Narratives of Ritual

### *Buddhist Symbolic Language*

The first intercultural consideration, one that became evident early in this process, is that the majority of the healers practice Tibetan (Vajrayana) Buddhism, a lineage that has an unusually rich and deeply held tradition of using symbols to describe the sacred. Tibetan Buddhism commonly refers to the layers of a symbol's meaning using the categories of *outer*, which refers to a physical level; *inner*, which refers to a spiritual level; and *secret*, referring to an intimate level of experience. Additionally, language achieves a greater density in meaning due to the constraints upon native Tibetan speakers' English fluency: The subtlety and depth of their philosophical understanding is necessarily compacted into simple English words.

For instance, the practitioner and healer Geshe Chaphur began his narrative with a reference to space: "Most important thing is, making space: inner making space." On an outer level, the theme of space referred to the use of correct breathing technique and the energetic alignment of the treatment room. Within the Five Element theory utilized by the majority of co-researchers, the element of space represented the client's consciousness: The mind itself is considered to be as vast as the open sky. As Lama Jinpa pointed out, the element of space interpenetrates the other four elements. On an "inner" level, this capacity of the space element symbolically describes the interdependent nature of consciousness and matter. Within Geshe Chaphur's Bon practice, "making space" also refers to the attainment of nondual awareness. This cultural understanding of "space" endowed his narrative with a deep and nuanced understanding of relationship, and a refined ontological view that expresses the deeper meaning of his praxis. These deep, interrelated threads of meaning do not render themselves visible to the casual reader when removed from the cultural context of the Vajrayana symbolic narrative.

## Linguistic Differences

The challenge of interpreting Buddhist ritual is both cultural and linguistic: The traditional Buddhist languages—Sanskrit,

Tibetan, and Chinese—do not yield themselves to a single meaning. Chinese language does not have verb tenses, or a way of stating (singular or plural) number; there are other grammatical simplicities as well. These multiple understandings require contextualization, because the co-researcher's ontological stance is expressed through these traditional Buddhist terms. The multiple translations of *Sowa Rigpa* are far more rich in meaning than our English equivalent (Tibetan medicine). Tibetan language allows for diverse, multilayered understandings of this phrase. Lama Tsering Ngodup, who served as a linguistic consultant, described the meaning of *Sowa Rigpa* in this way: *Sowa* can be understood as healing (e.g., healing of wounds, healing from dismay, broken bonds, and getting stronger through nourishment and physical exercises). *Rigpa* can be understood as art of, science of, or any skillful application that works in given situations and conditions.

However, an alternate translation of *Sowa Rigpa*, "the nourishment of awareness," was used to refer to Yuthig's *Nyingthig*, a seminal text on spiritual practice for Tibetan doctors that is the accompanying volume to the Four Medical Tantras by Dr. Chenagtsang (2014), a teacher of Tibetan medicine who referred to spiritual practice as the ultimate form of *Sowa Rigpa*, and to medicine as the relative form of *Sowa Rigpa*. Through the context provided by this linguistic dialogue, the reader can glimpse some of the issues and challenges of conveying these many-layered terms into English. For instance, one might not perceive Dr. Chenagtsang's understanding of the mutuality of the practical and liberative aspects of healing. If this term were conveyed without cultural context, the essence of the phenomenon being searched for would be lost.

The healers in this study are using Buddhist terminology, symbolic expression, and teaching, which originated in the linguistic-cultural milieus associated with Sanskrit, Chinese, and Tibetan languages: cultural milieus that embedded multiple layers of meaning within a text (Berzin, 2000). Within Tibetan Buddhism in particular, study is considered an essential prerequisite to the direct experience of phenomena through meditation; culturally, it is expected that the primary experience of students will be supported by the contextual foundation established by right understanding. In writing this book, the meaning embedded in healers' actions and healers' narratives needed to be rendered visible to the uninitiated. The healers' stories often assume a great deal of cultural knowledge and a great deal of knowledge of other materials.

## Characteristics of Healing Rituals

At the heart of all the stories of Buddhist lineages, in their descriptions of the path to enlightenment, we find the essential healing crisis of awakening, through which the three poisons of anger, desire, and ignorance are transformed through insight into medicine, so that the seeker himself becomes a great physician of the spirit (Birnbaum, 1979; Clifford, 2006; Zysk, 1991). We can interpret all Buddhist healing, symbolically, as a ritual of initiation, empowerment, and transformation (Vargas, 2003). For Buddhist traditional healers, the healing ritual is not only symbolic; the ritual is effecting an archetypal change of consciousness, and through this, catalyzing physical healing.

We can also view these rituals on an archetypal level that illuminates the healing process across cultures. Exploring Buddhist rituals, it becomes evident that these rituals are expressing something essential, for their practitioners, about what it means to be human: They are a primary way of making meaning of life, and finding a relationship to the world in the midst of the transformation and disruption of illness. The embodied narrative of ritual serves as a lens through which the healer's worldview becomes visible. Both these spoken and performed narratives can help us to perceive the ways in which the healer is calling upon the hidden wholeness that he or she perceives as the central organizing principle of life.

This deep function of ritual can be well understood through the work of Cheryl Mattingly (2004), the medical anthropologist. Even though we are primarily drawing on the healers' own ways of making meaning, there is something we can learn from the Western perspective. It can help us to make the connections between the healers' stories and the Western practices of healing that we commonly encounter—such as psychotherapy and medical checkups. In her work researching Western medical practices, Mattingly has described six key characteristics of healing rituals:

- There is a heightened attention to the moment, a "existential immediacy" which gives an authority and legitimacy to the activity.
- A multiplicity of sensory channels carry the meaning, sight, touch, sound, smell, creating a "fusion of experience."
- Aesthetic, sensuous, and extralinguistic qualities of the interaction are accentuated.
- The intensification of experience is socially shared, and it emerges through mutual bodily engagement with others.
- Healing actions are symbolically dense, creating images that refer both backward and forward in time—the patient is located symbolically in history.
- Efficacy is linked to potential transformations of the patient and sometimes a larger social community.

These characteristics, taken together, provide a working definition of healing rituals that serve as an entry point to the healers' narratives. We will see that each ritual we study is, indeed, so dense in meaning that entire libraries could be dedicated to their study. The narrative of each ritual provides the client with a sense of being supported by spiritual forces that reach into the distant past and to the future. These rituals provide a vivid embodied and relational liminal space, a threshold between the physical and archetypal worlds. Through this liminal space, the power of the present moment can be fully utilized for personal and shared transformation.

Given that our exploration of healers' stories is a doorway into a different cultural world, a world of contemplative and indigenous practices, it is essential to prepare ourselves for the art and science of translation. While all interviews were conducted in English, these narratives, in their telling, also included body language, pauses between words, and other contextual cues that cannot be replicated on the printed page. As one healer counseled, "it is necessary to listen for the spaces between the words."

Quite simply, Choga (ritual) is a path of accomplishing a goal; accordingly, we've organized our discussion of ritual according to its various goals. The goals of Buddhist healing rituals fell into these seven categories:

1. setting intention
2. mindfulness
3. creating space
4. therapeutic attunement
5. evoking sacred power
6. changing awareness
7. reconnection with the natural world and community

# Chapter 4

# Embodied Wholeness—Healers' Stories

In my research on Buddhist healers I focused upon Tibetan Buddhist practitioners, as the transmission of their healing lineages was, up until the mid-twentieth century, less complicated by sociopolitical factors. Within China, Cambodia, and Vietnam, Buddhist societies were reshaped to fit colonization, or the needs of an atheist state: Buddhist practices were considered bourgeois and a potential threat to the autonomy of the state. Acupuncture and other traditional healing practices were "reformed" by the Chinese government to retain mechanistic functionality; spiritual components of traditional healing were removed from the traditional medicine canon. While there are some reservoirs of traditional healing cultures within these countries, and to some extent, within émigré communities, traditional healing resources are more easily accessed within the Tibetan communities in exile in the United States.

Within the Tibetan community, cultural suppression and genocide began in 1950, with China's annexation of Tibet. In Tibet, traditional Tibetan medicine is now practiced and taught within the government's primary care systems in a rationalized and socialized form; traditional Tibetan medicine centers are subject to policy and budgetary pressure from Beijing. The Tibetan diaspora community has intentionally focused on the preservation of its traditional culture through education. As Tibetan resettlement in America has taken place, the energy, conviction, and philosophical depth of Tibetan cultural practices has been generously shared with the West. This cultural exchange has already brought about several generations of Tibetan Buddhist teachers and healers who are not of Tibetan ethnicity. The resultant ethnic diversity within Tibetan healing lineages is reflected in the interviews that follow.

The healers represented a broad spectrum of healing lineages and praxis. Several healers worked within more than one healing modality. Two were doctors of Tibetan medicine; two were acupuncturists; five worked with subtle energy; three worked both through ritual and ceremony, and through counseling. These five classifications (doctors of Tibetan medicine, acupuncturists, energetic healers, performers of ritual, and counselors) describe the full range of traditional Buddhist healing practice. This wide range of modalities reflects the syncretic nature of Tibetan Buddhist medicine, as it has entered into dialogue with other cultures over millennia. The acupuncturists had training in both Tibetan Buddhist and classical Chinese medicine. A Tibetan monk integrated Reiki into his Medicine Buddha lineage practice. A Chodpa (Chod practitioner) kept up a thriving homeopathy practice. This accurately reflects the cultural crossroads at which Buddhist traditional healing is situated in the twenty-first century. All were recognized by their communities as healers—sought out for pujas, traditional medicine and energy work, and counseling, and given various degrees and recognitions according to their lineage. I will now introduce these extraordinary men and women in greater detail.

**Geshe Chaphur** is a 37-year-old Bon Buddhist monk born in Amdo, Tibet. He was ordained at the age of 17, and has been teaching for over 20 years. Within the Bon Buddhist community, Geshe Chaphur performs Chod ceremonies to clear the karmic debt that is considered a contributing cause of illness. He also uses Tsa-lung practice (Bon breath-yoga), mantra practice, and energy rebalancing by means of the five elements to bring about healing. Geshe Chaphur's practice and scholarship have been recognized with several awards given by the Tibetan community. A translation of his Tibetan language texts is currently underway. Geshe Chaphur serves as the Guiding

Teacher of the Gyalshen Institute in Berkeley, California.

**Dr. Heidi Harding** is a licensed acupuncturist in her forties, based in New York state, and an experienced practitioner of Bon Buddhism. Heidi is of Anglo-American origin. Her path as a healer began when she experienced skin rashes that did not have any identifiable origin or effective treatment within Western medicine. Heidi had the good fortune to study with a classical Chinese medicine practitioner who was also a Taoist priest, the 72nd in his lineage, and through this mentorship, attain a deeper insight into the spiritual practice of acupuncture than is commonly available within TCM (traditional Chinese medicine), the standardized version of Chinese medicine adapted by the Chinese government after 1950. Heidi also integrates Bon soul retrieval, Tsa-lung, and Bon five elements healing into her professional practice.

**Dr. Devatara Holman** is a licensed acupuncturist whose path began during travels to Tibet and China as a spiritual seeker. She acquired fluency in Tibetan and Chinese languages in order to study Buddhism. Due to this fluency, she was asked to serve as an interpreter at a Chinese hospital, where she began to gain a deep appreciation of the healing arts. Devatara Holman is a Guiding Dharma Teacher in the Dzogchen lineage of the Nyingma tradition of Tibetan Buddhism, and a recognized Qigong Master in the Emei Linji Chan school of Chinese Buddhism. Devatara is an Anglo-American in her fifties; her office is located in Sausalito, California.

**Lama Jinpa** has been training in Tibetan Buddhism for over 20 years; he received the title of Lama upon completion of a three-year retreat. Lama Jinpa founded a school for the practice and study of Chod practice, which is considered a valuable resource by many within the Tibetan Buddhist community. He is also a homeopath and energy medicine practitioner. He has published several books about five elements healing theory. Lama Jinpa is of Anglo-American ethnicity. His office is located in Burbank, California.

**Christina Juskiewicz** has been practicing Tibetan Buddhism for over 20 years. She is ordained as a Buddhist nun; Christina trains and does healing work with Segyu Rinpoche, who holds the Segyu lineage of Tibetan energetic healing, a lineage connected with the Medicine Buddha. The Juniper Foundation is the nonprofit organization that carries this healing work and meditation teaching into the world. However, while Juniper Foundation is rooted in Tibetan Buddhist lineage, its approach is secular: The intention is to make these practices more approachable to Westerners. Christina is an Anglo-American in her early forties. Her exploration of Tibetan healing practices began when she experienced an energy imbalance during a period of spiritual exploration in India and Nepal, and was healed by Segyu Rinpoche. Christina currently serves as Vice President of the Juniper Foundation; their office is located in Palo Alto, California.

**Lama Tenzin Sherpa** is a Tibetan monk of Nepalese origin in his early thirties. His work as a healer began when he became ill as a young monk. His teacher used Reiki, mantra practice, and Medicine Buddha practice to support his recovery. While staying at a hospital, he saw many sick people and dead people; this gave him strong motivation to learn and share these healing modalities. Now Lama Tenzin Sherpa travels and teaches widely, using Reiki, Medicine Buddha practice, mantra, counseling, and Dharma teaching to bring about healing. Lama Tenzin Sherpa's home temple is located in New York City.

**Dr. Malcolm Smith** has been a practitioner of Tibetan Buddhism for over 30 years. Dr. Smith is Anglo-American, and in his fifties. Out of a deep interest in Tibetan Buddhism, he availed himself of an opportunity to take the 5-year course of study given to Tibetan Medicine doctors at the Shang Shung Institute of Tibetan Medicine. His instructor was Dr. Phutsog Wangmo, whose voice is also present within this narrative study. After completing his program at Shang Shung in 2009, Malcolm attended an internship at Tso ngon Tibetan Medical Hospital in Tibet and received the traditional oral transmission of the Four Medical Tantras from Tibet's most senior doctor, Aku Kyima. Upon completion of his studies, Dr. Smith established a practice in Ashfield, Massachusetts. Malcolm has completed a 3-year meditation retreat, and holds an Acharya degree in the Sakya school of Tibetan Buddhism. Malcolm also serves as the resident Tibetan Doctor at Siddhi Energetics, a Tibetan pharmacy, and is a member of the group practice Clinic Alternative Medicines in Northampton, Massachusetts.

**Dr. Phuntsog Wangmo** is a Tibetan Buddhist woman in her fifties. Her family came from Eastern Tibet, and they held some renown within the community; the family had several tulkus (reincarnations of Buddhist teachers), scholars, and senior monks. However, after the Chinese invasion of Tibet, "everything was turned upside down." Her brother became a doctor, and she also followed this path, studying through a program in Lhasa. After completion of her training, Dr. Wangmo came to the West and co-founded the Shang Shung Institute of Tibetan Medicine in Conway, Massachusetts with her teacher, Chögyal Namkhai Norbu Rinpoche. Dr. Wangmo continues to teach both in Massachusetts and internationally through the Shang Shung Institute. She is also a co-founder of the emergent American Tibetan Medicine Association.

# Chapter 5

# Foundational Healing Rituals

## Setting Intention

The first way is to remember the purpose of healing. To remember the Medicine Buddha or the spiritual master who taught me healing. (Lama Tenzin Sherpa)

For all healers, the practice of setting intention was integral to their healing work. Practitioners described the beginning of their work as a reflection upon its purposes: The Bodhisattva Vow (a vow of compassion, which is a commitment to be of service to all beings) and the lineages of healers and teachers were cited as pathmarkers in this process. The Bodhisattva Vow is cited in the Four Medical Tantras as a prerequisite to embarking on the path of Tibetan medical studies.

When we learned the medicine, we agreed to help sentient beings from suffering in whatever way we can help. (Dr. Phuntsog Wangmo)

It is considered to provide the healer with deeper reserves of energy, and greater capacity for effecting healing. (Dr. Phuntsog Wangmo)

I think the seed of the doctor is compassion. That is the seed. On top of that seed, then yes, you can help through knowledge, experience and so forth, and it becomes fully developed as a doctor. Without that compassion, you become like a business, like a mechanic. (Dr. Phuntsog Wangmo)

Just to get up in the morning and to be with people who are in physical pain, or emotional pain every day—for me, my Buddhist practice is essential...taking Bodhisattva vows every day and then creating that intention of "May I be of benefit to all beings..." if I didn't have that as a foundation, I'm not sure if I could do what I am doing every day. (Dr. Heidi Harding)

Allowing oneself to receive the support of these teachers made it possible for the healers to have a stronger consciousness and a wider energy field to work from.

Since this healing work is based on the interdependence of body and mind, the healer's own mind needs to be appropriately attuned. The wellbeing of the healer's inner world, his or her capacity to act with pure motivation and deep commitment as a vehicle for the transmission of healing energy, played a vital role in the creation of health. In fact, many of the healers considered the healer's intention as a powerful point of intersection between meditation practice and healing work.

It's one. It's completely one. Everything is absolutely interconnected. Every thought that I have affects myself and all sentient beings. That's my experience. That's the absolute view from which I work, from which I live my life. So I know that my thinking has the potential at any moment to be beneficial or harmful, to myself and to other beings. So, it's from that point of view that I'm able to utilize the very specific techniques that come from the world of Buddhism. (Dr. Devatara Holman)

Dr. Holman shared an anecdote from her personal experience that illustrated this point. As a Buddhist student and medical interpreter in China, she came across a book in the local bookstore, which described the correct way to move chi (energy) using acupuncture needles: One could alternately drain excess chi or tonify chi, based on the specific direction in which needles were rotated. The next day, during rounds at the hospital, she saw two Chinese doctors working together, on opposite sides of a patient, working on analogous points, working to produce the same effect, but turning the needles in different directions. Devatara was surprised by this, and inquired into the technique. The doctors responded: "If you know the answer to that, you know the answer to all healing." And the answer, of course, was "It is all in your intention; the method doesn't matter so much, but your intention makes all the difference." This story illustrated how integral an understanding of consciousness is to the practice of healing within the work of these traditional Buddhist healers. In considering the healing work at the level of consciousness, the setting of intention is complemented by the practice of attention: the practice of mindfulness.

## Mindfulness

Mindfulness is a key factor within traditional Buddhist healing: All healers considered mindfulness practice foundational to their healing work. Mindfulness can be defined as "the capacity for attending to the content of our experience as it becomes manifest in the immediate present" (Bodhi, 1998). This capacity for sustained, undivided attention is essential in the subtle pulse-taking and other diagnostic and treatment processes that are common to traditional medicine.

> Whatever we do, the doctor needs to be mindful. Whether you give moxa or herbs or reading the pulse, the doctor needs to be mindful. We say, body-mind-speech, you have to be completely present. (Dr. Phuntsog Wangmo)

Practitioners described the way they began their day, and individual treatment sessions, with mindfulness, working with the breath and with mantras to center themselves in the present moment. Knowing one's own mind, it then became possible to help clients achieve realization. Mindful breathing served as a source of renewed energy for healing work.

> We get energy from air. It is very precious. It is new life, new healing power. (Lama Tenzin Sherpa)

Breathing correctly made it possible for the healer to come into his or her work from a place of balance and connection, which is the natural state. This is already a healing ritual, and the healer's work begins with his- or herself. In the words of Geshe Chaphur, "Practice is healing. Practitioner is healer. ...Through this practice, you can heal your consciousness, your mind. Others and yourself: both."

Mindfulness made it possible for the healer to be present with his or her own body-mind experience, and also unconditionally present to the client and his or her experience, extending a quality of spaciousness and acceptance of the client and the client's condition. Through interpersonal resonance, this quality of "stillness, silence, and spaciousness" (Dr. Heidi Harding), as embodied by the healer, gave the client the opportunity to realign his or her body-mind to this place of wholeness and balance. This experience of mindfulness extended the client's capacity for integration by dissolving his or her pain, or supporting the client in finding spaciousness within his or her pain through the development of a broader self-awareness. As Dr. Harding noted, "We can see that the pain is not constant—that we are more than just our pain." In fact, she added, healing could be defined as this state of integration: "familiarity with stillness, silence, and spaciousness."

Within energy work that utilized the Tibetan subtle channels, mindfulness was the medium through which the mind effected physical healing: Consciousness, the breath, and the subtle channels were completely interdependent. Working with one's consciousness brought about a stabilization of the breath and strengthening of the subtle channels. Similarly, working with mindfulness of the breath brought about a stabilization and purification of one's consciousness by means of the subtle channels. These processes were inseparable. For practitioners who focused on physiocognitive (mind-body) medicine, the practice of working with clients' internal states to effect physical change, mindfulness made it possible for healer and client to change thought patterns that had created imbalance to more efficacious thought patterns. Dr. Holman described the process in both Buddhist and neurobiological terms: In Buddhist tradition it is recognized that the mind processes millions of thoughts within each instant. Each thought influences each cell within the body, through the catalytic effects of neurotransmitters and other neurochemicals; these then have a crescendo of effects upon the physical body, resulting in the need for physical intervention, at the culmination of this process of cause-and-effect. The most effective preventative medicine, or intervention to counteract the effects of negative cognitive patterns, is therefore mindfulness, coupled with intention.

Within discussions of mindfulness, healers often described its healing effect in terms of "removing grasping." Dr. Malcolm Smith described this process in detail, from the perspective of traditional Tibetan Buddhist medical theories. Within classical Tibetan medicine, the primary cause of all illness is the mistake of grasping at an individual identity. This incorrect grasping gives rise to three kleshas (poisons): desire, anger, and ignorance. Desire, anger, and ignorance then give rise to the three doshas (physical imbalances), which manifest physically through the full range of physical illnesses, depending on the client's predisposition. From this perspective, the meditation practitioner/healer treats the primary cause of illness by releasing this grasping at self-identity in oneself and others: This is experienced as a sense of inner spaciousness and freedom.

## Creating Space

The ritual of creating space carries different levels of meaning. To begin with, on an inner level, it refers to reawakening the sense of spaciousness and stillness within the practitioner's mind/heart. On an outer level, it refers to making a space sacred through ritual. All ritual activities in Buddhism can be considered to evoke sacred energies, and thus create a sacred space (a space identified as a manifestation of the sacred) (Hardy, 2014).

However, to understand the ritual of creating space it is necessary to inquire into the Buddhist concept of space, which was interwoven throughout participants' descriptions of the healing rituals of mindfulness and creating space, and also figured prominently in their discussions of five elements traditional medical theory. In Buddhist worldviews, a symbol will often carry several layers of meaning, each layer referentially located within the body of Buddhist culture and practice. Each layer reveals different aspects of the symbol, and may additionally express different levels of realization (Rinpoche, 2011).

Dr. Holman described the tenets that anchor the power of Buddhist symbols within the context of a discussion of the significance of the reference points of the five elements, and the element of space. Within this discussion, Dr. Holman described four levels of correspondences between the phenomena (in this case, the phenomena of the five elements) and the whole:

1.  All in One (All exists in One)
    The primordial purity of Buddha-nature exists within each one of us. Through this, we have immense capacity for self-healing.

2.  One in All (One exists in All)
    Every thought that I have affects myself and all sentient beings. Every aspect of self-cultivation and healing that I

achieve supports the endless numbers of sentient beings with whom I am connected.

3.  One in One (One exists in One)
    Each of us is complete, just as we are.

4.  And All in All (All exists in All)
    The totality of the macrocosm is greater than the sum of its parts. We exist within this totality like waves which rise up from—and ceaselessly return to—the great ocean. It is good to be part of this.

Dr. Holman also described the connection between the microcosm and the macrocosm: "As inward, so outward: as outward, so inward." These paradigms arise out of the Mahayana Buddhist worldview. In her work, they inform her understanding of the five elements model and the process through which information becomes stored in the body.

Tibetan Buddhism commonly refers to the levels of a symbol's meaning using the categories of outer, which refers to a physical level; inner, which refers to a spiritual level; and secret, referring to an intimate level of experience. On an outer level, when healers referenced the theme of space, it referred to the use of correct breathing technique and the energetic alignment of the treatment room. Within the classical Buddhist five elements medical theory, the element of space represented the client's consciousness: In Buddhism, mind itself is considered to be as vast as the open sky. As Lama Jinpa pointed out, the element of space interpenetrates the other four elements. On an "inner" level, this capacity of the space element symbolically describes the interdependent nature of consciousness and matter. This cultural understanding of "space" allowed healers' stories to achieve a certain density of meaning.

Most important thing is, making space: inner making space. (Geshe Chaphur)

The healers described meditation practice as a means to create inner space. Meditation techniques for creating space differed according to lineage. Many practitioners used mindfulness of the breath as a meditative focus; additionally, mantra practice was utilized as a meditational focus in tandem with basic mindfulness techniques. Through this ritual of creating space within, the healer was then able to offer the client a wide and open relational field. The ritual of creating space for oneself and the ritual of creating space for the client were different facets of one practice. As Geshe Chaphur noted, "I do the same thing when I do healing practice: through that energy I can make space (toward) trying to make the view more natural: Mind." Within Geshe Chaphur's statement, Mind refers to the ultimate space of nondual awareness.

## Mantra Practice
A mantra is a phrase that is repeated as a meditative practice to bring the mind to a state of concentration. Mantras may have specialized uses, for example to bring healing, or to connect with elemental energy. However, their central purpose is always to awaken the practitioner's heart/mind (Blofield, 1977).

Mantra practice was considered by all practitioners to be a precision tool for linking the physical and mental bodies, through the focused energy of speech and breath. Within the Buddhist "three gates" model, body-speech-mind that is a traditional Buddhist formulation of complete openness, speech mediates between the realm of the physical body and the realm of consciousness. Mantra practice encompasses themes of intention and mindfulness: It is a precision tool within many Buddhist healing traditions for accomplishing the goal of directing intention and attention towards specific healing outcomes. Healers considered the mantras as vehicles for specific archetypal energies. Every healer utilized these in their own spiritual practice, many incorporated mantra into their healing sessions, and some invited clients to employ mantra within their regimen of self-care to effect their own healing through a shift in consciousness. The repetition of mantra supports the development of *samatha*, mental concentration, which results in stabilization and clarity of mind: an experience of sacred space within the body-mind.

In certain Vajrayana practices, the three gates of body-speech-mind are a multilayered symbol that, on an inner level, refer to the three kayas (three bodies or three orders of reality, as described in Chapter 2). While many of the practitioners agreed that the three kayas are a good working model of the connection between the body and consciousness, within their communities these kayas are often considered to denote an enlightened state. However, the framework of the three gates did not carry that added significance. Therefore, within the Tibetan Buddhist community, the model of the three gates is a culturally skillful way of discussing the connections between consciousness, intention, and the physical body. Within this framework, breath is symbolically connected with space. On the physical level, breath is a tangible way of creating space within, so that healing can take place. On the inner symbolic level, speech (which includes breath and more specifically, mantra) archetypally transports the healers' energy and intention from consciousness to the physical body, and the place where healing is directed.

Within our community of healers, those working within the Tibetan Bon lineage used the most extensive mantra practice, including the seed syllable "Ah," connected with the element of space. By reciting this mantra, they participated in a traditional breath yoga, which opened up the spaciousness of deep abdominal breathing as well as the spacious nature of mind, the ground of being (Rinpoche, 2002, 2011).

"Ah" syllable is the essence of space. So you just say, "Ahhhh." Through this sound: sound syllable, energy all of them are together. Then you can make open your mind, because you can open your space. Your space is unlimited. (Geshe Chaphur)

## Returning the Mind to the Heart

Within the Buddhist healing paradigms that work actively with the classical five elements system, there is a correlation between the creation of space, and the centering of the mind within the heart. The theme of reconnecting mind and heart was evident, illustrating this concept of embodied sacred space in significant and powerful ways.

The heart is the space element. So if you're returning someone back to their heart then that means they are really connecting with that spacious quality within themselves. And that space— that's where healing happens. And sometimes creating space is that allowing. ...Usually, when we have pain or illness, we tighten around it or we want to push it away. We don't accept. But just in that allowance, that is space. ...When a person is in touch with that space, they're free. Everything can be healed when one experiences that (inner refuge of stillness, silence, and spaciousness). And I think all of that—the acupuncture points have the potential, if they're the right points at the right time, done in the right way and there's openness of the person, then they can really help create that stillness, silence, and spaciousness for a person who may never have experienced that before. And then it is a very profound, deep experience. People can always go back to that. ...Healing is a familiarity with stillness, silence, and spaciousness. That's inner refuge. And then you become the medicine that's available for yourself. (Dr. Heidi Harding)

In Tibetan culture, this emphasis upon returning to the heart is a central narrative, expressed through the mantra Om Mani Padme Hum, which is literally translated "May the jewel reside in the lotus," a metaphor that is most directly interpreted as, "May the mind rest within the heart." This mantra is associated with the Bodhisattva Vow (the vow Tibetan doctors take to relieve the suffering of all beings, a core element of the Mahayana Buddhist path). This emphasis upon creating space within the heart is congruent with practices of classical Chinese medicine, in which the heart is considered to be central to all physical and emotional healing. There was a mirroring evident in healers' descriptions of meditation practices, as a ritual of creating space within, and their preparation of the treatment space.

> I begin my day with meditation practice there, by making offerings, blessing the space and trying to be very aware of my mind. (Dr. Heidi Harding)

The creation of sacred space can be seen, then, as one action with two aspects: the external and inner experience.

## Medicine Buddha Puja

This process of ritual preparation for healing is mirrored by the Medicine Buddha Puja, a core Mahayana Buddhist meditation practice associated with healing lineages that was already established in the first centuries of the Common Era and is still widely practiced today. A *puja* is a devotional ritual that is comprised of offerings to an enlightened being and meditation practices. The Medicine Buddha Puja begins with practices of setting intention: restating the Bodhisattva Vow to be of service. Within the introductory text to the Medicine Buddha Empowerment, the theme of releasing one's grasp on intrinsic existence, so as to see and understand dependent origination, is underscored through the practitioner's recitations. There is also an invocation of the lineages of awakened beings and teachers, with special attention to the lineage of Medicine Buddhas. The practices of recitation of mantras and liturgy in the presence of these lineages bring an "existential immediacy" to the practice of mindfulness. The creation of space is taking place through mindfulness; it is also given a tangible form through the puja's mandala offering. Mount Meru, which serves as the axis mundi of the Tibetan archetypal universe, is visualized with jeweled palaces, flowers, and other representations of beauty, sun and moon, and offered to all sentient beings. This sacred ground prepares the way for what Tibetan Vajrayana practitioners refer to as the creation stage, in which the Medicine Buddha is visualized with the traditional attributes associated with this Buddha. One healer described the effect of this visualization in terms of resonance, a neuropsychological process. Visualizing an awakened being stimulates in the practitioner an empathic awareness of his or her capacity for centeredness, clarity, and insight. That wisdom and beauty resonates within our mind and body as if it were our own.

Prayers and meditations follow, which support the practitioner in the development of openness and appreciation. The puja then culminates in a final visualization: The Medicine Buddha dissolves within the practitioner's heart. This awakened energy is then rededicated to the wellbeing of all sentient beings. As one healer counseled:

> This concept about the human body (as sacred space) is very deeply embedded within Tibetan medicine. The best shrine room you have is right here, between your two ribs: the center of your body, your heart. (Dr. Malcolm Smith)

This puja, together with other ritual practices, strengthens the connection between the physical body and the sacred, and imbues the physical body with sacred power so that the healers' insights are not only cognitively understood; they are thoroughly embodied: Through this embodied knowing, the healer has the capacity to access a level of insight which can only be grasped through direct experience. Within the sequence of healing rituals, it is through the creation of sacred space that the ground is then established for therapeutic attunement.

## Therapeutic Attunement

That dialogue, that interplay between patient and practitioner, between heart and mind, for both of us — is the first treatment, the first way of moving chi. (Dr. Heidi Harding)

Within all the healers' stories, the theme of therapeutic attunement was underscored. Therapeutic attunement can be described as the healer's capacity to "focus attention on others and take their essence into (their) own inner world" (Siegel, 2010, p. 34). The importance of relational connection was underscored in healers' accounts of their initial meeting with the client, and their intake interviews. Healers considered the establishment of a good relationship with the client to be paramount, as that relationship would serve as the vehicle of healing. When asked about the connection between the healer's vision and the client's process of healing, Devatara Holman described the healer's vision as integral to the healing process. The healer's vision provides the psychospiritual template for the therapeutic relationship: It serves as the first step towards the creation of healing:

First of all, they must understand their own goodness, because a lot of their suffering comes from not recognizing their own goodness. Of course, their suffering comes from not recognizing their own true nature, right? That's where all of our suffering comes from. It's pointing them in that direction — and also establishing some ground rules for where we want to go: what kind of relationship we are going to have.

[To begin] I establish with the patient that I recognize their primordial purity. And they need to recognize that also. The reason they are suffering is that they do not recognize that themselves and therefore feel separated. They don't know themselves—which is another way of saying they don't know their own thinking—I recognize their primordial purity and by virtue of seeing that, it already grows. That establishes the ground of our relationship. They know that I am always looking at their best part. That's the center for a positive relationship. And, they must then look for that in me, as well. Because they know I am looking at them in this certain light, and [guiding them along the path to healing], they are then obligated to follow that path and [hold their relationship with me in that light]. They will cultivate faith in themselves, in their positive thinking, in what they're experiencing, what they receive or feel me doing. There is therefore a mutual trust. And they're less likely to feel insulted or begin to feel like they need to rebel. Compliance is no longer so much of an issue from a clinical point of view. (Dr. Devatara Holman)

What, then, is required to establish this connection? The treatments began, in all cases, with a short intake, inquiring into the causes and conditions of the clients' imbalance. During this initial intake interview with the client, healers asked their clients questions about their day-to-day relationships with significant others, their community, and the environment. The strength of these relationships was considered a fundamental component of the client's state of illness and wellness: It mirrored the client's relationship with his- or herself.

Many practitioners also included the practice of taking the pulse, which in classical Chinese and traditional Tibetan medicine involves great nuance, and requires deep attentiveness. Within the ritual of therapeutic attunement, there was a sense that the healer was simply reflecting back the client's wholeness. Implicit within this expression was a belief that the client already possessed the wholeness and clarity that are the seeds of healing; this awareness had become obscured by inaccurate perceptions of oneself and the world. Devatara Holman made a practice of introducing traditional descriptions of that wholeness and clarity to new clients, so that in hearing those phrases, the clients would begin to see and recognize these mirrored attributes within themselves. Additionally, Devatara Holman, Lama Jinpa, and others worked simply with the active use of intention and attention, to establish an awareness within the client of the doctor's perception of these qualities within them. This established the ground for a strong therapeutic alliance. Through the healer's capacity to hold this vision of wholeness for the client, these practitioners reported that healing began as the client entered the room; that this practice of clear perception had an inductive effect upon the client. In the words of Lama Tenzin Sherpa, "When they see love, they get love." The therapeutic relationship is the matrix of healing. The client's confidence in this relationship supported the development of trust in the healer and treatment modality; it also strengthened compliance with the treatment regimen. The strength of the therapeutic relationship catalyzed a positive healing outcome. Then, ultimately, this capacity for healthy relationship will be integrated throughout the client's life. Dr. Holman stated:

> We hope that when they are a little further down the line, that every relationship is a healing relationship. I hope to support people in having a healing experience out of their life. Not just with me, but to make life itself a healing experience.

This ritual of presence is already bringing the client into a place of integration.

This natural and deep correlation between sensory awareness, self-awareness, and empathy is described in Buddhism through the concept of rupa-skandas. In the words of Dr. Malcolm Smith:

> The rupa skanda is made up of ten things: it's made up of your five sense organs, and five sense objects. Right now, you and I don't consider that we're sitting in the same room [we are on Skype]. But we're actually, at this moment, sharing the same rupa skanda, because we're both acting as visual and auditory objects of one another. It is profoundly nondual if you really understand what abhidharma's actually talking about. What they're saying is, if you go and strike somebody, you might be hitting someone else's body, but you're effectively doing violence to your own rupa skanda. So when I am treating a patient, I am not just treating a patient, I am also treating myself. That person—now they're in front of me—that means they're part of my rupa skanda. I'm part of their rupa skanda. This is where the language of self frays badly at the edges. (Dr. Malcolm Smith)

The role of the therapeutic alliance in restoring a sense of integration cannot be overstated. This process of creating a strong and healing therapeutic alliance is strengthened by the healer's practice of embodied presence, the healer's capacity to be at one with the totality of who they are and who the client is, with particular attention to their physical being and emotions (Ray, 2009). Within Buddhism, that practice of embodied presence is an expression of interdependence: the essential unity of body and mind, inner and outer experience. The healer's connection within his or her own body/mind provides the foundation for empathic resonance, a sense of safety and containment. In the words of acupuncturist Heidi Harding:

> We are...creating an open space, where people can allow themselves to be seen. I think a lot of the work is just bearing

witness to people's experiences, people's pain. Creating an openness—just that openness in the sacred space together—is very powerful. (Dr. Heidi Harding)

The role of compassion in this work is central: as Dr. Wangmo stated, "the seed of the doctor is compassion."

Within the context of hospice work at a meditation center, this restoration of relational connection was a powerful experience that brought one healer to reconsider the root meaning of healing. The hospice accepted clients from every cultural background, many of whom had no previous connection to Buddhism. However, in the course of their time at the hospice, these clients had the opportunity to enter into therapeutic relationship with community members who provided palliative care, including spiritual direction, in a deeply meaningful way that facilitated self-reflection. For some hospice clients, this experience of therapeutic relationship was deeply transformative: One reported it was his first and only experience of receiving such care. These connections created some measure of emotional security, through which clients were able to acknowledge and work consciously with their dark emotions, coming through this to a place of acceptance, forgiveness, and restored relationships. In many cases, clients' expected lifespan was extended by weeks, months, or in one case even years, time the clients successfully used to bring their life relationships into a healed state of connection.

## Evoking Sacred Power

While the attunement with the client was itself a powerful healing ritual, many of these healers also evoked sacred power to support the client's recovery. Within Tibetan medical systems' consideration of the various dimensions of health and illness, the potential effect of karma (past actions) is considered as a proximate cause for certain kinds of illness: This effect is remediated through meditation practice and ritual.

As a simple practice of accessing the support of the numinous, many traditional healers recited the Medicine Buddha mantra during their treatments. Several traditional Tibetan healers cited the use, in especially difficult cases, of the meditation and visualization practices connected with the enlightened being Vajrasattva, which are connected with purifying moral and ethical lapses.

## Vajrasattva

Vajrasattva is the Tibetan Buddhist Bodhisattva whose aspect of Buddha nature is that of purification. *Vajra*, in Sanskrit, refers to both a diamond (in indestructibility) and a thunderbolt (in force). In Vajrayana Buddhism, the Vajra is a symbolic image and ritual object: a full description of its symbolic meaning could easily encompass a book of its own. In short, the Vajra is a diamond scepter which symbolically represents spiritual power and upaya, skillful means. *Sattva*, in Sanskrit, denotes a being. This powerful being, Vajrasattva, is visualized as pure white, seated in lotus posture, holding a vajra and a bell. (Clifford, 2006)

The meditation practice associated with Vajrasattva (commonly called Vajrasattva practice) follows the same inherent structure as the Medicine Buddha Puja, in the practices of mindfulness, setting intention, and creating sacred space. This is a practice the healer generally assigned to the client for his or her spiritual practice, rather than performing the ritual on the client's behalf. The client-practitioner visualizes the awakened being, Vajrasattva, above one's head, imbued with grace and nondual wisdom. There is then a practice of calling to mind one's negative actions, expressing regret, and calling upon Vajrasattva to assist in breaking through this pattern of suffering. The practitioner then visualizes Vajrasattva's light filling his or her body, cleansing body, speech, and mind. Negative imprints and impurities are visualized as creatures, dark ink, and other unpleasant forms that are naturally removed, just as dirt is cleansed by water, or as darkness disappears in the presence of light. One then sets an aspiration to refrain from negative action in the future, and envisions Vajrasattva merging into one's body.

There are many levels on which this ritual may effect healing. First, the acknowledgement of negative patterns, in the context of connection with a source of awakened energy that then helps shift these patterns, resolves the existential anxiety of illness as well as the quotidian stress that affects health-related behaviors and the immune response. During serious illness, clients have an especially strong need for connection with the numinous. The clarity of Vajrasattva is symbolically granted to the practitioner through the dissolution of Vajrasattva within the body, which then may serve as a source of confidence and resiliency: This naturally counteracts the sense of isolation and disempowerment that often accompanies illness. The ritual provides a safe container, within which the client can consciously engage the psychospiritual crisis of healing and the raw power of dark emotions. When the container is established, a recitation follows: The client surrenders to accept the unwanted experiences of life and makes meaning of these in the context of cause-and-effect. As the client calls upon Vajrasattva for assistance, this act of surrender helps him or her release the contraction of ego defenses in order to make contact with an interdependent self that is in contact with, and not separate from, the numinous. Through the visualization, the client makes conscious contact with unpleasant physical feelings and dark emotions by locating them in the body. This conscious work to befriend the dark emotions supports the development of affect tolerance, which leads to greater resiliency. Through meditation the client is led to explore negative emotions with a spirit of recognition and acceptance; this constructive self-reflection makes it possible for the energy and emotional insight that underlies the dark emotions to become conscious. Finally, this ritual helps the client attend to, and resolve, the existential challenges that illness presents by putting this crisis in the context of the path of awakening.

## Chod Practice

In order to experience fearlessness, it is necessary to experience fear. (Trungpa, 2007, p. 33)

Several practitioners described Chod as their preferred ritual for cutting through obstacles in cases that were otherwise intractable. Given the intricacy of the formal Chod ritual, many healers referred clients to a Tibetan lama who then performed the Chod ritual. The Chod ritual is among the most complex Tibetan Buddhist ceremonies: Its liturgy interweaves complex and nuanced sacred music and meditation rituals with an experiential visualization. In the interest of precision, it should be noted that there is not one, but several Chod rituals. Chod, as a practice, developed syncretically out of the practice of Indian Buddhist adepts, the revelations given to Machig Lapdron and other Tibetan Buddhist siddhis, and through the cultural infusion of indigenous Bon practices. These different sociocultural contexts give rise to differing nuances of understanding within Chod. Here, I will briefly delineate the core aspects of Chod ritual found across Tibetan lineages.

As with all Buddhist healing rituals, Chod begins with the expressed intention to be of service; in this case, the path of service is explicitly stated as cutting through the attachments to the body and to the self (Phabongkha bde chen snying-po, 1984). While the Medicine Buddha Puja and Vajrasattva rituals referenced begin with taking refuge in the support of awakened beings, the Chod ritual begins with the practice of awakening compassion. Thrangu Rinpoche described the reason for this inversion:

> Chod is a special practice. Its purpose is to enable practitioners to pacify and overcome emotions, especially the strongest emotions that disturb and harm most painfully (pride, anger that is born from hatred, passion, ignorance and jealousy) as well as those feelings that are not listed as the most harmful emotions but that arise due to attachment to a self (such as fear, depression, etc.). Therefore it is necessary to open one's heart to others every time one engages in the practice of chod by first generating bodhicitta. (Rinpoche, 2006)

The practitioner then performs a series of preliminary practices. Sacred space is created through the ultimate offering: The practitioner's body itself is the microcosm/macrocosm that is offered to the benefit of all beings. This practice sets the tone for the entire Chod ritual: By offering the universe through the human body, the practitioner shifts his or her self-identity from that of a person with limited resources, to that of a field of blessings, infused with spiritual power (Sorenson, 2013). The central Chod practices then follow.

**Phowa.** The first of the central Chod practices is Phowa. In the presence of awakened beings, the practitioner envisions the negative patterns that have caused illness or other obstructions. These patterns are then cleansed by the awakened beings and the Great Mother (representing the womb of totality). This psychospiritual element is roughly analogous to that described in the Vajrasattva meditation, in which negative patterns are experientially acknowledged in the context of connection with, and surrender to, a source of awakened energy that then helps shift these patterns. The mindstream (consciousness) is then released from the body through an energy channel that terminates at the top of the head, and returns to the source of being. The contraction of ego-defense is released through this archetypal experience of death, in order to renew the primary connection of the self with the numinous. This practice supports the release of ego-clinging and the development of detachment with regard to the physical body.

**Tonglen.** The second of the central Chod practices is Tonglen. Tonglen meditation consists of the practice of taking on others' suffering and sending out wellbeing (Novick, 1999). This inverses the habitual mode of seeking relief, in which one seeks to remove suffering and receive wellbeing. Through this inversion, the ego defenses are overcome, and a deep, more resilient connection with the interdependent self is realized. In Chod ritual, Tonglen takes on the greatest existential immediacy: One's own body is the substance offered to the archetypal shadow forces of the psyche, described within Buddhism as the three poisons (desire, anger, and ignorance). These shadow archetypal energies may be referred to as *lhadra*, god/demons (Brown, 2013), using a more indigenous interpretation, or as *dud*, mentally fabricated negative forces (Sorenson, 2013), within an Indo-Tibetan Mahayana lens. The archetypal energies feast first upon the body in the form of life-giving nectar, and then again upon the body as blood, viscera, and bone. The directness and psychic intensity of the lived experience of Chod sacrifice brings the practitioner into vivid nonconceptual contact with the essential power of the archetypal exchange of self and others through the sacred space of the body. This intensity is heightened through the haunting sound of traditional Chod melodies used to summon the *lhadra*, played upon *kangling*, trumpets constructed from human thigh bones; the *damaru*, a hand-drum which represents primordial emptiness; and other dedicated instruments. The instinctual fear that arises in practitioners through this ceremony is contacted consciously, and used to cut through self-grasping. Geshe Chaphur stated the purpose of Chod succinctly:

> What is healing? Take out the problems and make happiness. When I am doing Chod practice I imagine that everything is being taken out, as an offering. I do not desire anything. I do not desire to have problems, or take away problems. I have no desire there. No grasping. Because you cut through your negative emotions, your grasping...feelings are joyful. (Geshe Chaphur)

While the ceremony is too elaborate to be performed by a single healer, certain healers cited short adaptive visualizations that were integrated in the course of a treatment as necessary. In addition, the visceral, direct nature of the Chod ritual trained the healer to bring this focus and immediacy to his or her work with clients.

> It is supposed to be a lived experience. ...With real healing you have to get in there, get your hands dirty, have a direct experience of what is going on with that person: what their limitations are, what their blocks are, what their karma is, et cetera, and then come up with solutions that are also based on symbiosis, based on interaction. (Lama Jinpa)

### Bon Soul Retrieval

You can sometimes see that in the person's countenance— they look almost in shock, pale—or you don't see that life is really being cultivated. So in my tradition we would say that the soul qualities in the elements are not relating to each other. You would then look to see what element is out of balance and then try to retrieve that and strengthen the life force. (Dr. Heidi Harding)

Tibetan Bon practitioners referenced soul retrieval as another practice of evoking sacred power. Within their traditional healing practice, clients who are lacking in vitality may be diagnosed with the energetic condition of soul loss. Tibetan Bon practice utilizes a five element model to describe the primordial energies of the universe as well as the energies of body/mind (Rinpoche, 2002). The elements of earth, air, fire, water, and space are considered to undergird both spiritual and material existence. In experiences of trauma, there may be an experience of disassociation: Traditional Bon healers describe this disassociation as the displacement of an element. The healer can retrieve that element using mantra and a visualized and kinesthetic process, through his or her connection with the five elements within their own body, and their connection with that element in nature.

Through my words, the essence goes to the element, then trying to bring wind. Bring the fire. Bring earth. Bring space. ...Through my mantras, power goes to the elements, then brings energy back. (Geshe Chaphur)

These healers reported state changes in their clients, including the dissolution of blood clots that were confirmed by Western biomedicine.

Other practices of evoking sacred power utilized by the traditional healers in this study included the evocation of Dharma protectors, fierce aspects of the archetypal energies of compassion utilized within Tibetan meditation practice, in tandem with the use of mantras. Through the repetition of sadhana, these visualizations arose spontaneously in the midst of healing treatments. With the incisiveness of a surgeon, the wrathful archetype was visualized cutting through imbalanced areas within the client's body, so that the body could regenerate.

Having connected with these powerful archetypal energies through formal ritual, the experienced practitioner can then harness his or her energies according to the therapeutic needs that arise in the moment.

## Changing Awareness

First the consciousness changed, and then the body changed. I feel that that's really important. I think that's what happens. (Dr. Heidi Harding)

On an ultimate level, the efficacy of all these traditional healing practices could be ascribed (within the Buddhist worldview) to a change in awareness. This meta-ritual took diverse forms, ranging from direct insight into the nature of mind through somato-emotional shifts effected through acupuncture, subtle-energy work, and the traditional rituals of Medicine Buddha, Vajrasattva and Chod. All of the healers agreed that changes in awareness were central to the experience of healing. On a primary level, that change of awareness involved the clients' development of right understanding with regard to the causes and conditions of their illness. Healers described paths of inquiry with their clients that encompassed diet, sleep, relationships, environment, and spirituality, as well as other holistic concerns. This counsel did not follow a prescribed script, but evolved naturally in conversation with the client, in tandem with the client's innate understanding.

Usually people have a sense of what they need to change but they just need some guidance. Because—if you want your symptoms to change, you can't be at the same consciousness as your illness. So often it does really come from either changing one's perception of oneself or situation or their illness and— yes, really changing one's mind. (Dr. Heidi Harding)

This narrative is in accord with traditional Buddhist medical theories, as described earlier in this chapter: Illness arises out of the mistake of self-grasping; healing is based on illuminating this obscuration, and freeing oneself from the prison of self-cherishing in order to rediscover a healed and interdependent connection within one's relationship with the self, others, and the natural world.

> You have this basic state of "I" making, "I" and "mine," which the Buddha taught us so well, this is our basic problem in samsara. This causes the three afflictions. (Dr. Malcolm Smith)

The imbalances in one's environment are, through interdependent arising, mirrored by imbalances within the body. By working with the client to develop self-insight and to bring his or her lifeworld into balance, these distant and proximate causes of illness are addressed. For clients who are Buddhist, specific meditation instructions might be given.

> Tibetan medicine we say, is sMan. SMan does not mean only the herbs, pills, moxa, needles: sMan means, benefit. So whatever can benefit is medicine. So the physical body needs to take the herb supplements, but the energy body needs to be treated a different way. ...Understanding the three poisons, recognizing them, understanding the value of life and then including understanding of impermanence, and so forth: I think this is one of the fundamentals to preventing disease or treating disease. (Dr. Phuntsog Wangmo)

Several Tibetan doctors referenced the Medicine Tree that is used to illustrate the path of Tibetan medicine. Within this traditional *thankga* painting, the various pathways to illness and wellness are shown as branches of a tree. The uppermost part of the tree depicts a Buddha image inside a rainbow, conveying the essence of Tibetan medicine as a path to awakening. However, all of these traditional healers also acknowledged the different belief systems of their clients, and described their readiness to adjust their counsel accordingly to a secular practice of mindfulness.

Sometimes I am sitting with a patient who is taking herbs with me and I say to them, maybe you can sit this way, and then breathing—because you don't have to be Buddhist. Also: this doesn't have any side effect. So this way, I sit with them and show them how to do together, to breathe, to stretch, certain things. I do this quite often. (Dr. Phuntsog Wangmo)

All my patients are not Buddhist. I do not teach them all these things. I just say to them "breathe well." So I teach how to breathe, how to calm mind, how to remain present: all those things. They need to know their own breathing. If they do not know their own breathing they do not know their own life, their own attitude. The more they connect with their breathing, the more they will connect with themselves. (Lama Tenzin Sherpa)

A change in awareness was also effected through the use of acupuncture needles.

I feel like the work I do is often just helping people to create more of a sense of awareness and spaciousness. And then, the acupuncture that I do is the ritual of that: it helps integrate that. (Dr. Heidi Harding)

This state of integration is characteristic of mindful awareness; in addition, some healers described the shift of awareness within healing treatments as a nonordinary or altered state of awareness, akin to shamanic states of consciousness. One healer averred that the roots of acupuncture practice were located in indigenous traditions of stewardship of the Earth. This healer, as well as others, acknowledged that acupuncturists trained today in Tibetan and Chinese medicine are not often trained in the depth of spiritual cultivation that makes this subtle application of acupuncture praxis possible. However, many practitioners of Tibetan and Chinese medicine described the goal of their acupuncture, bodywork, or energy-clearing technique as moving energy, which then effects a change of consciousness towards increased awareness, "initiating real consciousness where it's obscured."

Healers described this shift as a return — a kind of homecoming, a return to original nature, a self-recognition of the innate completeness, which was not dependent upon physical conditions. This return to a natural state of integration, centeredness, and in-dwelling enabled the client to bring disorders of the body and mind, as well as life situations, into balance.

This theme of return was often accompanied by the motif of resting the mind in the heart.

> The spirit rests in the heart, like a nest. The heart is like a nest. So if the mind and the spirit come back to the heart, then the body can heal itself. (Dr. Heidi Harding)

The rituals of effecting change of consciousness worked in tandem with the rituals of creating space; many healers described these as simultaneous, interwoven experiences.

> First, the consciousness heals, or returns, or reawakens, and becomes enlivened. And there's a sense of spaciousness that one experiences. Then the healing is possible. Sometimes the healing is in that shift of consciousness. (Dr. Heidi Harding)

While some scholars (Mumford, 1989; Wilber, 2000) have averred that Buddhism is concerned simply with healing consciousness, and working on this ultimate level, all of the healers in my study were unanimous in their commitment to effecting healing on both relative and ultimate levels. Some healers contrasted this pragmatic approach with the common presentation of Buddhism in the West, which is often solely focused on the development of nondual awareness.

You need to work at both levels. Everyone has their own problems, physical, mental, anything. So, better to remain at both levels: the ultimate level and the relative level, so that we can provide our service to everyone. (Lama Tenzin Sherpa)

## Reconnection with Relationships

Through supporting the client's achievement of this natural state of integration, the healer also facilitated the client's restoration of healthy relationships with his or her community and the natural world. This experience of healthy connection was as central to the healed experience as the restoration of body-mind integration.

Everything is important. When people have a concept of self-dependent, that is the main cause of problems. They become self-centered, self-separate, which creates self-centered action, which creates division and which becomes completely unnatural. So communities also suffer, people also suffer. Because everything is interdependent, everything is connected. This is why healing work is both healing the self and healing others. We see the self in relationship to other people. Every thought, every action, whether physically or mentally—every action should be beneficial for both. We need both sides. Not one winning, one losing: one gaining, one not gaining. That is natural community, the natural law, the natural state. (Dr. Phuntsog Wangmo)

For this reason, within traditional Buddhist ceremonies, including Medicine Buddha and Chod ritual, many clients simultaneously receive the benefit of healing in the context of community. Dr. Eduardo Duran, a Native American psychologist who uses mindfulness in working with Native American communities, uses ritual and ceremony as a way to work with an entire community. He considered this the most expedient means given the urgency of the need for individual and collective healing:

> There's the fact that we're not separate. If one individual is suffering—in most of the communities I work with, the whole community is suffering. And so it makes sense to address it. ...If we just do only one person at a time, as in given Western models of individual psychotherapy, I guess it's a good thing—but we're running out of time, I think, and we need to do a little bit more. And traditional healing circles—like in the Indigenous world—most healing ceremonies are done publicly, so that the whole community can come, and there's no separation. Then the community can help hold the energy for the healing. It's for an individual but since the whole community's doing it, they're healing also.

This worldview is in good alignment with Buddhist perceptions of interrelationship: *Paticca samupadda*, the interdependent arising of phenomena, is applied equally to the individual's condition of health and the collective state of wellbeing. By supporting the client's development of insight into the roots of wellness and illness, the healer is providing both preventative medicine and cure for the wider body of the community. As Devatara Holman noted, within the one, there is the all. Lama Tenzin Sherpa's insight fits seamlessly along these same lines.

> If one person's health is clear, that also helps the other person...when we heal one person, that means we are

helping not only one person: many people. We are helping through their family, their friends, also. This is basically why when we heal one person we are giving benefit to that other person also. This is why, if a person is not healthy, not happy, always everyone should know why there is this condition. For example, if people are not accepting of the present condition, not happy with their present condition, they will develop illness: physically, emotionally, mentally. The present condition is the result of past condition. And the present condition is the cause of future conditions. This is why everyone should know what I am doing. (Lama Tenzin Sherpa)

## Healing Rituals: Summary

I have used the embodied language of ritual as a way to grasp the healers' stories. Those intrepid readers who have familiarity with the trails of the Southwest may know of riprap, loose stone used to provide a foothold on steep trails, or along streambeds. Within our exploration of Buddhist healing practices, the embodied language of ritual is serving as a kind of riprap through which the lay reader can find a foothold within the cultural context of their healing work. Although each Buddhist lineage has its own particular healing rituals, we are working across lineages, to identify the meta-rituals that unite these practices. This will permit us to connect with the wider field of research, to examine spiritual transformation and healing across cultures. The meta-rituals we identified were (a) setting intention, (b) mindfulness, (c) creating space, (d) therapeutic attunement, (e) evoking sacred power, (f) changing awareness, and (g) reconnection with the natural world and community.

Intention, the focused application of thoughts and energy towards a certain healing outcome, prepares the foundation for the healing treatment, and is continually extended throughout the healer's work. Mindfulness supports the healer's intention with the application of attention, so that the healer is "completely present" (Dr. Wangmo). The healer releases his or her own grasping, so as to be a vehicle for healing. The theme of nongrasping is most dramatically expressed through the healing ritual of Chod; however, it is a key element of healing performed by both healer and client. This is in line with Buddhist medical etiology, which considers nongrasping the cornerstone of health. Through the application of intention and attention, the healer is able to mirror back the client's wholeness; the theme of mirroring wholeness was active within healers' accounts of the intake process, and active within certain healing rituals. By mirroring the client's wholeness, the healer instills confidence and a sense of agency and positive potential in the client, which supports the client's active participation in the healing process. The integrative element of healing described as returning the mind to the heart was present in all narratives, and served as an element in most healing rituals. Another key element of Buddhist healing process, change of consciousness, was also present within all narratives and the majority of healing rituals. Reconnection with the natural world was often described through work with the five elements: These served to bring about the integrative experiences of changes in consciousness and the return of the mind to the heart. The power of relationships in the process of healing was woven throughout all healers' accounts of their work. The establishment of the therapeutic relationship was supported by intention, mindfulness, and nongrasping. As healers reflected back the love and wisdom they saw within the client, this established the foundation through which the therapeutic relationship could achieve its potential. The therapeutic alliance then prepared the client to discover the pure potential of relationships within his or her community and environment.

As we look closely, to see the connections across the healing rituals and varied modalities, space served as a meta-theme.

Just as, within Buddhist medical theory, space is considered to interpenetrate the other elements, the theme of space was present within all rituals. Space described the experience of attunement with intention and mindfulness; the attitude of nongrasping; the positive ground of potential generated by mirroring wholeness and generated by creating healthy interpersonal relationships. Space (in its representation of consciousness and of emptiness) served as the medium through which *tendrel* (cause-and-effect) connected all things. When we speak of cause-and-effect, we are describing the causal mechanism through which these various practices (intention, mindfulness, nongrasping, reflecting wholeness, elemental energies, and relationships) brought about the return of the mind to the heart and changes in consciousness.

## Rituals and the Lens of Anthropology

In Chapter 3, we looked into the qualities that Mattingly (2004) identified as characteristic of healing rituals. By revisiting Mattingly's description of ritual, we can place our understanding of Buddhist healing within a cross-cultural framework. We can see that these rituals tap into an archetypal awareness we all possess, which is part of our human nature and closely bound together with our ability to heal.

Mattingly noted these five aspects of ritual: "existential immediacy"; range and depth of sensory experience; aesthetic experience; socially shared experience, with bodily engagement; symbolic density; and potential transformation. Within the meta-rituals we have examined, the practices of setting intention and mindfulness heighten "existential immediacy" (Mattingly, p. 75). Traditional healing rituals of pulse-taking, acupuncture, moxa treatment, provision of herbal medicine, and meditation practices amplify the "aesthetic, sensuous and extralinguistic" (Mattingly, p. 75) elements of the therapeutic experience. The quality of deep relational attunement within the therapeutic dyad is intensified by bodily engagement. While this connection may take place one-on-one or in the context of shared ceremony, its effectiveness is explicitly linked to personal and social transformation.

# Chapter 6

# The Five Elements in Healing (Lama Jinpa)

In order to place the wisdom of these healers in context, it is essential to understand Five Element theory, which dates back to at least 500 BCE. Five Element theory provides us with a particular map of the human body in relationship to the natural world, based on a traditional understanding of interdependent arising: There is no separation between the individual and the natural world: its macrocosm is mirrored in the microcosm of the human body/mind. Thus, Five Element theory provides a tangible model through which we can track the workings of cause-and-effect within mental, emotional, and physical healing, within various traditional medicine systems. The Buddhist healers who I worked with perceived a dynamic connection to the natural world through the five elements of the client's physical body — which they considered to be the source of physical and spiritual vitality. In the words of Geshe Chaphur:

> Our body comes from the five elements: the water element is connected to our blood. The wind element is connected to our breath. The earth element is connected to our flesh. The space element is connected to our mind. The fire element is connected to our heat, warmth. So all the time, we say our body comes from those elements, living in those elements, dependent on those elements. Finally, we are dissolving into those elements. So all the time, we are just playing in the elements' playground.

We may also consider these case studies that incorporate Five Element theory into healing practice, provided by healer Heidi Harding:

Sometimes you can see where one element may be weak or hidden. That may manifest in emotions and it also can manifest and be visible through illnesses that people have. So, for example—there was one client who had a blood clot. This was a person who was having difficulty with their blood, which is ruled over by the kidneys, the water element. By retrieving from the universe, that water element and energy, and bringing that back to the body, the person was able to dissolve the blood clot. It's really pretty miraculous. They had been told by their physician that they would always have that: they would need to be on blood thinners. This was very dangerous. It was something they would have to live with. But, through just seeing this weakness in the water element—and bringing that back—change happened. The body really responds when those forces of the water reawaken, and they are re-invited.

That deficiency could also be seen by a lack of confidence; even though on the surface it seemed that they were very successful in their life and doing very well, there was a deep lack of confidence that is also an aspect of not enough of the water element.

So for that person it went hand in hand. Bringing the water element back, everything changed: their physical body changed, the quality of the blood changed, and then their experience of themselves changed.

**Resting the Mind within the Heart.** The picture, in both Tibetan medicine and classical Chinese medicine, is bringing the mind to rest back in the heart. The heart is like a nest for the consciousness. The first thing that I do, too, when I take someone's pulses, is I look to see the stability and the regularity in the pulses. And if there're variations between the pulses—between the right and left side of the pulses, or if there's a change in how fast or slow, if it speeds up or if it skips a beat, those are indications that there's some kind of separation from the person's mind, or that the mind is not resting in the heart. And that can happen.

The Chinese classics say that the spirit—the shen—are like little birds. They can get startled very easily, from a loud sound or something that happens in the environment. They can fly away. And that happens for people.

Sometimes I'll use that very imagery. And you can feel then, that there's an opening. People feel that their experience is being witnessed. They say, "Yes, that's what I feel like. I feel that part of me has left." The first treatment will be to stabilize the pulses: to return the shen, the spirit, back to the heart so that the spirit rests in the heart, like a nest. If the mind and the spirit come back to the heart, then the body can heal itself. But that regularity—the mind, the consciousness has to be stable, has to be resting in the heart. And that is the same in Bon tradition and in classical Chinese medicine. First and foremost, the mind has to be resting in the heart.

The Five Element paradigm of healing as a state of integration within oneself and the natural world is a signature expression of Buddhist worldviews and healing praxis. The healer serves as intermediary between the client and the natural world. The processes of healing are effective in that they restore right relationship and balance within the natural elements both within and around the client.

We are honored to present the teaching of Lama Jinpa, a scholar-practitioner with expertise in Himalayan Five Element theory, within this chapter dedicated to Five Element healing theory and practice.

# THE FIVE ELEMENTS: A NEW PARADIGM IN ENERGY HEALING

## Introduction

Vajrayana Buddhism, birthed and nurtured in the subcontinent of India from the fourth to twelfth century CE, found a comfortable home in the snowy ranges and isolated valleys of Tibet. There, with waves of transmission over several centuries, a unique mix of tantric theory and practice flourished and evolved into a highly sophisticated and complex vehicle of spiritual development. From its origins in the matrix of Hindu, Buddhist and shamanic practice, it developed a uniquely effective and practical system of personal transformation. And whole worlds, social and cultural, were constructed around that uniqueness. But at the very core of this intricate living system of worship and inner development there is one idea, one discovery, that runs like a golden thread through the entire massive construction. And that is the principle of the Five Elements: Earth, Water, Fire, Air and Space.

With its origins tracing back at least 5000 years to Indian Vedic, Egyptian and Babylonian sources, the Five Element model of reality is one of the oldest and most persistent ideas in human history. Yet in that long journey, it has acquired its share of barnacles, bumps and bruises. It has been in turn truncated, distorted, misunderstood, appropriated, modified beyond recognition, and finally ignored as obsolete superstition. Yet it persists, in various forms, pure and altered, because it is simply one of the most profound universal truths ever recognized by an ever-questing humanity. Our purpose here is to show the way in which these profound truths have functioned within Tibetan Vajrayana. And then to indicate how that can be translated into our modern idiom, beyond the confines and limitations of any single religious tradition or cultural setting.

## The Breadth of Five Element Concepts

There are many threads to follow in weaving together the fabric of Five Element theory. This includes Hindu sources (particularly the Samkhya system), Ayurveda, the long-lasting Greek interpretations, numerous European mystical traditions, and modern contributions of Steiner, Jung, and others. Yet the best place to start is the sophisticated repository of Elemental technology, which is Vajrayana Buddhism. Here the Five Elements have a central importance, not as some abstract cosmological theory, but in literally hundreds of *practices* that work directly with these formative principles. The following list is not meant to be exhaustive. But certainly it will give a sense of how much Himalayan Buddhism, as practiced today in Tibet, Nepal, Bhutan, and all over the Western world, is pervaded by this one central idea.

## The Five Buddha Families (*rig nga*)

The Five Buddha Families are at the core of Vajrayana Buddhism, representing the enlightened or fully purified form of the Elements. The goal of the entire path of meditation, mantra, ritual and purification is to convert our mundane five-element consciousness *and* body into the purified five-partate Buddha mind and Elemental light body.

## Mandala Iconography

The Tibetan mandala is a template of perfected being. The thousands of such diagrams and paintings are based on a wheel with a center and four "spokes" in the cardinal directions. This is the floor plan of a visualized three-dimensional fortress of enlightened mind. Space usually resides at the center, with the others laid on in the cardinal directions, the four quadrants of the Buddha families. The home of deities and sub-deities, this cartography takes on a whole new meaning when we realize that this same map can be applied to "ordinary" psychological mind, both in its healthy and disturbed states. Likewise, it can be used as a healing map for our physical body. We should note however that the psychological and biological usage of the Five-Elemental mandala or floor plan is simply absent from traditional Himalayan Buddhism.

## Empowerment

Empowerments (*wongkur*) are essential requirements for undertaking the tantric practices that include deity visualization, mantra recitation and Tsa-lung—work with the energy channels and chakras. Each and every one of these thousands of empowerments is a transmission of Elemental energies (white, red, blue, yellow and green) from a higher spiritual source to the corresponding Elemental centers of ourselves, as mundane receivers. This seed is to be watered and nurtured by one's own practice, in order for it to grow to its full potential. That fruition is none other than the Five Buddha Bodies, five different realms or levels of spiritual existence and expression.

## Yidam Practice

The central characteristic of Vajrayana is the visualization of oneself as a luminous enlightened form, a deity with a specific kind of form, attributes, color, mantra, and enlightened mind state. But this is always part of a full grouping—either visualized or assumed—of a center figure and four Elemental complements. Next, there are typically Five-Element light offerings that radiate from the mantra in the heart of the deity. These rays strike various Buddhic pure realms, followed by a reciprocal transfer back as a purified stream of five-color spiritual force. The primary goal here is enlightenment, not mundane status, success, life abilities or even a healthier body or mind, though these may occur as a natural by-product of this activity.

## The Four Activities

However, there does exist a genre of ritual that focuses on the Elements (four of them at least) in order to improve one's lot—ostensibly only to support one's spiritual journey. These practices use, in sequence, Earth for enriching, Water for purifying, Fire for drawing in, and Air-Space for eradicating. Using mantras and what amounts to standardized affirmations, the rituals are designed to make various enhancements to mundane life—Elementally.

## Long Life Rituals

Using a symbolic arrow with five-colored silk banners, rituals are used to avert obstacles to premature death, and to gather life-prolonging energies from the entire universe. Along with visualization and mantra, the arrow is twirled in such a way that the Five-Elemental life force and vitality is drawn in and condensed as five-colored lights. These forces may also be concentrated into doughy pills, and ingested—or kept for later life-threatening emergencies!

## Dakini: Female Wisdom Beings

Dakini practices are different than Yidam meditations, as we do not visualize ourselves in their form. Instead, five external goddesses, representing the condensed essence of the Five Elements, bring us healing and spiritual boons in the form of sequential lights, forms and mantric sound. These unique feminine wisdom expressions of the Five Buddha Families recur as a main theme throughout Vajrayana, as heralds of the coming good.

## Healing Rituals

Within the thousand-year-old tradition of Chod, or Cutting Through, are a series of healing rituals that rely wholly on the Elements. With elaborate liturgies, music and visualizations, participants are cleansed of defilements and negative karmic imprints, while the pure elements are reinstated—an Elemental oil change. These are also performed effectively for groups of sick individuals, who remain lying down during the practice. In all cases, the Dakini or Feminine Wisdom Beings of the Five Families are prominent figures.

## Shangpa Style

Within the Shangpa Kagyu lineage of Tibetan Buddhism is a group of unique self-healing methods. Transmitted in our era by Kalu Rinpoche, shapes and colors of the elements are used, the meditator merging with this meditation object. After going through the Elements in order, from Earth to Space, they dissolve one into another, emulating the stages of dissolution at death. Another remarkable Elemental healing set is the meditation on the Empty-Ah, in the variations of the great Tibetan sage, ThangTong Gyalpo. These purifying "empty body" practices are designed to counter excesses of heat, cold, wind, and so on, by washing the body through with its opposing Element.

## Land Healing

Vajrayana has extensive methods of environmental remediation, which involve balancing the Elements. Chö rituals, for example, can remediate earthquakes, floods, fire, droughts, and other natural disasters. The present Dalai Lama's famously successful rainmaker, Lama Yeshé Dorje, used these very practices. The same rituals are often used for plagues and epidemics, considered to be related to Elemental disturbances, often personified as earth spirits or demons, rather than microorganisms.

## Offerings

In the most ubiquitous use of Elemental "technology," every ritual, and most meditations within Vajrayana, have a section where infinite offerings are made from a primordial soup of the Five Elements. After first transforming the impure elements of mundane existence into their primary components, anything can be fabricated through meditative focus. Here, one basically offers the coarse Five Elements, made pure through meditation, back to the enlightened Five Elements, in the form of enlightened Yidam, Protector, Dakini or Buddha. This emulates our own inner shift, where the sullied components of body-mind are transferred back to their original pristine nature.

## Directional Offerings

In rituals of both personal healing and land purification, one addresses both the obstacles and the possibilities arising from the four directions and center. These are, quite naturally, correlated with the Elements, their colors, and their qualities. The Windhorse offering, for generating personal power and good fortune, often uses the intermediate directions as well— each having a corresponding deity. Such directional offerings are also primary to every known spiritual tradition and practice, from Brazilian *brujo* to Babylonian Magi.

## Demonic Entities

Finally, demonic forces, however one wishes to interpret them, are seen as belonging to the Elemental or directional families with which we are now familiar. In this case, their noxious influence corresponds to a particular kind of obstacle or sickness. Nagas, for example, control the forces of Earth and Water. They figure largely in the creation of natural disasters, but are also the cause of human illness, including immunological conditions and cancer. Hypersensitive to impurities of all kinds, they are incited to vengeful action by the polluting of land and sea. This is food for thought, as chronic illness escalates in tandem with our despoiling of the environment and damage to the ecology of our fragile green paradise.

Having a sense of how intrinsic the Elements are to the whole system of Vajrayana, it may come as a surprise that there are no dedicated or detailed texts, nor an oral tradition, explaining the various properties, characteristics, psychology or dynamics of the Five Elements. Modern teachers have made a step in remedying this problem, but these efforts are pioneering at best, have significant theoretical errors, and are still hide-bound by the framework of Buddhist hermeneutics.

## An Integrative Approach

Thus, there are valid reasons why we need to broaden our Elemental horizon. In spite of its rich and varied use, much Five Element information and practice remains fixed within the much larger ecosystem of Himalayan Buddhism. Whether it is an empowerment, land healing, deity meditation, or any of the topics listed previously, they are intertwined with a vast range of religious and cultural concepts. Part of the issue here is that the Vajrayana context always involves ritual and liturgy. Their length and complexity varies tremendously, requiring years of study and practice to become proficient, and sometimes a full day to complete! Even the simplest, however, has a well-defined structure and formula along Buddhist theological lines. Removing Elemental practice from this ritual context is essential. Not only is it not necessary for body-mind healing, but it allows a more accurate understanding of how the Elements actually work within us.

## The Cross-Cultural Matrix

The other compelling reason for thinking outside the Vajrayana box is that there is a rich mosaic of Five Element information scattered across time and culture, just waiting to be accessed. For a full and accurate application of Five Element work, it is imperative to integrate the unique knowledge contained within Ayurveda, Hindu Samkhya, Greco-European, and Bön traditions, to name a few. After all, if the Elemental model is indeed an accurate reflection of reality, then modern physiology and psychology should be easily transposed into the Elemental paradigm. In fact, this approach has already yielded striking new insights into age-old and as yet unresolved issues about human health and human nature, relationships, good and evil, male and female polarities and much more. On the flip side, this integration brings important advances to the otherwise culturally fixed and ritual-embedded Five Element principles within Vajrayana. Putting that puzzle together over a 30-year period, and validating the findings in meditation trainings and with individual patients, reveals a rich field of study that will take many generations to complete.

To discuss the extended world of influences that augment our Elemental knowledge would require several volumes. Each tradition seems to focus on one or another aspect of the full Five-Elemental picture, and each has omissions and sometimes outright errors. Here we can only briefly mention a few prominent pieces of the mosaic.

## *The Tattvas*

The non-Vedic Samkhya system of ancient India, commencing around 500 BCE, appears to be the first to write about the reality of subelements, or elements within elements. I had already made this discovery myself, when I found out that I was some 2500 years too late! The Tattva system describes the Fire of fire, Water of fire, Air of fire, and so on, such that there are 25 components in this first order of subdivision. This becomes very practical in terms of Elemental diagnosis, both physically and psychologically. It also demonstrates how Elements within Elements—continuing down into third, fourth, etc. levels of subdivisions—are the basis of our infinitely varied world.

## *The Greco-European Line*

Pythagoras was the great genius who brought the classical Asian ideas of the Five Elements to the West, primarily from India, but also from Egyptian and Babylonian sources. However, within a century of the violent eradication of his order, the great fifth element of Space was lost. And so the materialistic systems of Aristotle and Hippocrates would last for another two thousand years. Nevertheless, even missing its center, and a fifth of its meaning, the Humoral system that persisted into the modern era contains much useful information and the beginnings of a true Elemental Psychology.

## Ayurveda

The ancient Athur Vedic literature of 3500 years ago is our first inkling of an already well-developed Elemental healing system. Focusing on excess and deficiencies, displacements and distortions of the Five-Elemental forces within the body, they yield a rich resource, not found within spiritual systems. In later revisions the Five Elements are replaced by a truncated three Guna system to describe the body, as well as medicinal substances such as plants, minerals and animal parts. However, the original, more comprehensive Five Element tradition still exists within Thai or Buddhist Ayurveda.

## Homeopathy

A striking addition to our Elemental knowledge is the massive amount of information contained within homeopathic theory and clinical experience. One of the fundamentals of homeopathy is the discovery of five primary patterns of susceptibility or *miasms* that underlie all symptom patterns—and all disease. These correspond precisely to the Five Elements. Homeopathy is a medicinal practice and not a meditative or energy healing system. Yet the wealth of information it reveals about Elemental pathology of mind and body is infinitely more detailed than the observations of Vajrayana, Ayurveda, or the Greco-Roman traditions combined. Here is an astounding confirmation of these ancient truths, considering that homeopathy's founder strictly rejected these old-fashioned notions!

## But What Are Elements?

From here we can present a very rudimentary Five Element schema. Then we can describe how this translates into a new and unparalleled system of self-healing, treatment, and personal transformation. But before that, we have yet to define what an "element" actually is! When used in Tibetan Buddhist, Ayurvedic or other healing systems, we often see the term "elemental energies" or even "the five wisdom energies." But this is both a misnomer and a misunderstanding. New Age and Bioenergy Medicine alike have tended to call everything that is non-material or beyond physicality, a form of energy. Without a long discussion, we can simply point to everything in nature, and everything produced by humans. Yes, object and processes are formed of both matter and energy, but that form and its function is governed by principles, meaningful patterns, or what in the computer world are called "operating systems." The Elements are exactly that. They are the directives, the command-line structures that influence both matter and energy. In the body we see this carried by DNA and RNA, while Systems Theory looks at the complex mathematical models in living and non-living models. Biosemiotics investigates the signals and directives within systems. What we are looking at there is the top-level supersystems, not far from Plato's forms or archetypes, and Sheldrake's morphogenetic fields. The Elements are fixed programs, whose structure was already pointed at by Pythagoras in his five geometric solids (wrongly attributed to Plato!).

## Elemental Biology and Psychology

Next, the relationship of body and mind needs to be clarified. There is a whole field of Elemental psychology, based on what happens when one is not in touch with their authentic self, whose anatomy can be accurately described as the Five Ways of Power. There are states of disconnect, the Five Ways of Loss, and states of distortion, the Five Ways of Shadow. This is an effective and extremely profound method of personal change and psychological healing. But the balance of our physical Elements also affects emotions and attitudes. This is the "constitutional" aspect of the Elemental body—how excesses and deficiencies impact the mind. Here we have a clarification of the common confusions about the interaction of psycho-somatic and somato-psychic influences.

## A Brief Elemental Primer

The listing of Elemental attributes that follows does not touch on excesses and deficiencies of mind or body, but simply sketches out the main positive characteristics.

### EARTH

**Body:** Form, structural strength; connective tissue, bone, muscle, immune competence and disease resistance; stamina.

**Mind:** Stability in work, relationships, internal world, security; status within society, career, finances; practical, down-to-earth.

### WATER

**Body:** Suppleness, flexibility, flow; the vast aqueous biochemical sea of the body; interactive biochemistry, nourishment, detox.

**Mind:** Connection, intimacy, sensitivity; sense of care, compassion, responsibility; holism, nourishing relationships.

### FIRE

**Body:** Cellular metabolism; Krebs cycle; body thermodynamics; biological drive, purpose; oxidation and purification; catabolism.

**Mind:** Purpose and goal-directedness; clarity and focus; persistence and overcoming of obstacles.

AIR

**Body:** Motility and mobility; communication and information exchange; coordination; vitality and reactivity.

**Mind:** Creativity, expression; action and manifestation; resourcefulness and adaptability.

SPACE

**Body:** Biological intelligence; body coordination, endocrine balance; cavities of the body; storage of *chi* or *prana*; memory.

**Mind:** Integration, harmony, balance and hierarchy among different mental and emotional functions; wisdom, knowingness.

## Working with the Elements

### Physical Healing: Elements and Subelements

After what was said earlier, it may seem odd to talk about Elemental "energy" healing at all. This is further complicated by the fact that, among the Five Elements of Tibetan Buddhism, only energy (*rlung*) is described as having five-fold division, as five kinds of winds or sub-energies. However, as the Tattva system demonstrates, all the Elements have such subelements. The reality is, that working with human bioenergy is one of the most direct ways to access the operating system that is informing those circulating energies. In fact, energy is separate from that OS, and there are numerous layers and kinds of energies that are in play. This is something that literally all current forms of energy work have omitted. Over time, we have developed a system of forty Five-Element Energy Healing meditations (eight times five), using the appropriate colors, sounds, forms and concepts associated with each Element. The result is a comprehensive and deeply powerful system of self-care, impacting body and mind equally.

## *Healing Others*

These same ancient techniques, modified to fit a therapeutic situation, can be used as an effective healing system. Working with the hands, on and off the body, the practitioner uses their own inner visualizations and mental focus, asking the patient to also meditate on various colors, mantra, locations, or ideas. Using their energy sensitivity, the clinician discovers, with precision, the area, Element and type of disturbance that is currently the main obstacle to overcoming illness and promoting optimal health.

## *Psychological Healing*

Integrating important truths missing from both mainstream and pop psychology, Five Element Psychology is a unique and innovative form of personal change. The immense tower of Babel of modern psychology can be neatly reorganized and recoded, producing an elegant and effective way to understand, with accuracy, what is hindering our happiness and development. Self-treatment consists of a series of Elemental meditations, using color, forms and mantra, combined with special affirmations along the lines of Cognitive Therapy.

## Conclusion: A Modern Take

The potential for bringing Five Element meditations, visualizations, mantra and Tibetan yoga into a modern context is tremendous. Ancient principles and methods, simplified and streamlined for a modern audience, create rapid physical and psychological benefits that build over time. It is the ideal system of self-help, working directly with the very foundational structure of the psyche. It is also the next logical step in the now widespread practice of mindfulness. Those methods bring people to present-awareness, yet provide no map as to where to go from mere states of flow or relaxation. Elemental theory and Elemental practice is that very map, the long sought-after template of the human soul.

## Chapter 7

# Healing Rituals for Our Modern World

*An earnest ceremonial practice is like a magnet that aligns more and more of life to its field; it is a prayer that asks, "May everything I do be a ceremony. May I do everything with full attention, full care, and full respect for what it serves." Charles Eisenstein (2019)*

In the modern world, which is always changing, we need a way to step into sacred time, and through this, find that essence which is unchanging, and timeless. Ritual is a way of stepping inside the wheel of time, and looking at our life with a broader vision. Within the spaciousness and stillness of ritual, we find the center of the circle of life. Out of this centeredness we gain clarity, resilience, and a sense of deep meaning. While the rituals we have described are rooted in Tibetan Buddhism, we can touch into the healing power of ritual through these spiritual practices that have been adapted for contemporary life.

## Space-Creating Rituals

To create sacred space, traditionally one would offer a mandala, representing the ultimate sacred space, the wholeness of the universe, with the intention that all beings experience these pure realms.

In this version, we are envisioning our room, or house, as the sacred space.

The traditional manner, in Korean Mahayana Buddhism, would be to evoke the temple guardians. We have adapted the ritual for secular use.

Envision, at the south corner of your room, a golden rose. Now, see, at the west corner of the room, another golden rose.

Envision a golden line connecting these two. Moving to the north corner, envision another golden rose. See, again, a golden line connecting this to the golden rose at the west. Now, envision a golden rose at the east corner, and see golden lines connecting this to the north and south corners. See each of the four golden roses become a pillar, extending deep into the Earth, grounding the room. Now, see an additional set of roses, at ceiling level, at each of the four corners, connected with a golden line to each other, and to each of the roses at the base of the room, forming a golden cube. Now, create sacred space by evoking the guardians of the four directions. Some people may be most comfortable envisioning these as angels, still others as Bodhisattvas, and for others these energies may be known as impersonal archetypal forces, "winds" of the South, West, North and East. (These guardians of the four directions are featured prominently in Korean Buddhist *taenghwa*, altar paintings; in addition, the four winds are lauded in Korean Buddhist chanting.) Envision all those people who have carried a wish for your wellbeing, as well as those spiritual teachers that carry a wish of wellbeing for everyone. See their love and compassion like golden light, streaming down from them, filling every cell of your body. Allow yourself to fully receive that love. Join them in that intention, sending lovingkindness to yourself. *May I be filled with lovingkindness. May I dwell in joy and safety. May I have deep and natural peace.* Then, extend this to everyone in your community, everyone in the world. *May all beings be filled with lovingkindness. May they dwell in joy and safety. May they have deep and natural peace.*

## Ritual for Returning the Mind to the Heart

The traditional ritual for this is, most simply, mindfulness. When the urgency and commotion of everyday life presses upon you, take an intentional pause. Feel the breath, within the body, extending through the lower body, through the feet into the ground. Bring awareness to any place within the body that you may be feeling tension. Breathe through that tight place—whether it is the shoulders, the lower back, the brow—breathing spaciousness into whatever feels tense. Place a hand upon the heart, asking yourself, *what is going on for me right now? Can I be with it completely?*

## Rituals for Therapeutic Attunement

To attune to another, first complete the ritual for creating sacred space, and the ritual for returning the mind to the heart. Then, envision, around you, a perfect circle, within which your body is at the center, with a radius of a few feet. Envision, around the second person, a perfect circle, within which their body is at the center, and within which there is also a radius of a few feet. Envision the center of each circle set at the circumference of the other. See, where these two circles overlap, an almond-shaped area. Within sacred geometry, this is traditionally called a *vesica piscis*. Sense, within this point of overlap, the interconnection of your *nama rupa* (form and sensory experience) with that of the other person, the interconnection of your subtle-energy body with that of the other person. Take a moment to be present with that; acknowledge that connection. Then, enter into conversation, sourcing from that connection.

## Rituals for Purification

We all make mistakes. When we have a sense of guilt or shame with regard to a mistake we've made, this can obstruct our healing. This is an adaptation of a traditional Buddhist purification ritual.

Envision your highest potential—your grace, your inner light, your connection to the divine—as a brilliant, blissful white light, directly above your head. Imagine, for a moment, that that is the only moment you have to live. (In an ultimate sense, this is, after all, true.) Facing this basic truth, that death is certain and the time of death uncertain, generate a sense of regret, and an intention to purify your path.

Now, envision that presence of grace as a bright, powerful shower of light, flowing from above your head, flushing out any heavy or incompatible energy within your body/mind/ spirit, seeing that heavy, dark energy leave through the pores and openings of your lower body. Envision that dark energy being absorbed and mulched by the Earth itself. See that brilliant energy purifying every aspect of your physical body, then purifying your speech, and completely illuminating your mind. With this newly awakened heart-mind, generate an intention to be of service to others, wherever you find yourself in the course of life.

## Healing Rituals

When the foundations of our physical health are shaken, it can be profoundly beneficial to connect with a force greater than ourselves. In Buddhist tradition, one would call upon the Medicine Buddha to support healing on all levels. Here is a secular adaptation of that ritual.

Above you, envision a brilliant blue light, a blazing blue lapis-lazuli color, which has the quality of compassion and awakened energy, the source of peace, the source of life itself. Envision the guardians of the four directions (see above ritual, for creating sacred space), at the four corners of your room, creating a beautiful sacred space, which is absolutely safe, and within which you can deeply rest. Repeat the traditional Medicine Buddha mantra (Teyata Om Bhekanze, Bhekanze, Bhekanze, Maha Bhekanze, Bhekanze, Raja Samudgate Svaha) 108 times—envisioning that blue light descending from above your head, into your heart, and through the heart into every part of the body, illuminating every organ, every cell of the body with its brilliant lapis-lazuli blue healing light.

## Memorial Rituals

It is particularly important to learn Buddhist memorial rituals because, as a culture, we have forgotten how to grieve. Our society is organized around perpetual youth, and infinite expansion. In nature, however, seasons of expansion are followed by seasons of contraction. When the fullness of the harvest is complete, the leaves turn red, fall to the bare ground, and dance in the autumn wind. It is good to be part of all this. In order to work with these cycles consciously, we need to set time and space to grieve our losses. If we do not consciously grieve, then the natural passage of these cycles is arrested, and a part of us lives in the past with the unprocessed grief.

Here is one valuable ritual, adapted from Tibetan Buddhist *phowa* practice, which is an element in the Chod rituals we discussed earlier.

We can perform this ritual for ourselves, when we face a transition, to experience a deep letting-go. We can also practice this with a loved one as a way of helping them to die consciously. We can do this on behalf of a loved one, envisioning them within this sacred space at the time of their passing, or within our meditation practice at some later time, as a way of coming to closure.

We begin by connecting with our breath, practicing mindful awareness so that we are centered in the body and clear in the mind. Envision yourself as whole and strong, radiant, joyful— in some place which is beautiful and reminds you of the sacred. Above us is the source of love, wisdom, radiance, Buddha nature... whatever name we may give to it.

Whoever needs to forgive us has done so. We are extending forgiveness to whoever there is to forgive. If we like, we can use these phrases:

For all the harm I have done to others, knowingly or unknowingly, forgive me.
For all the harm others have done to me, knowingly or

unknowingly, I forgive you as much as I can.

For all the harm I have done myself, knowingly or unknowingly, I forgive myself.

Through this we experience a cleansing of the heart-mind.

The source of love—the one pure and clear thing—is so touched by this that the light from above radiates into and through us, entering our heart, suffusing through our body, our arms and legs, our toes and fingers...and finally our head.

We are completely filled with light. We have become that light, one with the source of joy, one with great love and compassion.

## Chapter 8

# The Clients' Work, and Clients' Experiences

While the focus on ritual has provided a useful lens through which Buddhist healing praxis can be seen in the context of relational ontology, the principle of *paticca samupadda*, interdependent origination, requires a more exacting examination of the process of healing. Given that healing, like all phenomena, arises in the context of interrelationship, the activity of healing cannot be solely located within the healer; the process was also dependent upon the client. I had some vivid experiences of this bidirectional process when completing the interviews for this book. Several of the healers engaged the author in dialogue, asking their own questions about the nature of illness and wellness in order to bring about a mutually constructed, shared awareness— letting the medium convey the message. Other healers simply articulated the need for conscious healer-client partnership within their stories: The client needed to trust the healer, and align him- or herself with the healer's work, in order for the client to receive the full benefit. Otherwise, the client might not recognize the positive effect of the treatment, or unconsciously work against it.

In the words of healer Devatara Holman:

Healing always is dependent on the patient. Even if Buddha was here, Buddha could only help them twenty percent: the rest is their responsibility. My capacity to help the client is determined by the openness and commitment that the patient has. I will do my work, but they need to follow through: they need to walk the path as well. They need to be responsible for at least fifty percent—and later on, more like eighty percent. Their willingness and determination are key. Some people just cannot slow down enough, or they cannot conceive of the kind of healing that might be possible for them. That limits their ability to heal, it even limits their capability to listen. The whole endeavor is dependent upon their ability and their determination.

In many aspects, the client's work paralleled the healing rituals of the healer. The practice of setting the intention to be receptive and work towards healing was paramount: "they need intention, they need the will, the deep interest to be healthy." This simple tenet is not always easy for clients to practice; several described interactions with clients who were not committed to their own progress, perhaps due to a secondary gain they experienced from their illness. In some cases, this ambivalence could be met through the development of the therapeutic relationship across time.

It was also very valuable, within the process, that the client themselves practiced mindfulness—and through this, created space for healing to take place.

"When will I get that result?" some people say. That depends on you, how you are able to make space yourself. If you can make space yourself, you can experience many things, like compassion, and lovingness, kindness, openness— everything, you can put in space. But, as a beginner, first of all it is a little bit difficult: space is small. So, first of all, need to make space bigger. Bigger means, to do practice. To do meditation. Just as much as you can. (Geshe Chaphur)

The client could apply pressure to some of the acupressure points designated by the healer, as a self-treatment, and was often expected to complete the course of an herbal prescription with diligence. The client could be given Kum Nye or Tsa-lung exercises to complete daily: These Tibetan yoga practices help to recalibrate both the subtle body and the physical body, and restore the flow of energy. Additionally, the client needed to "check their own life," to actively engage this process of self-reflective insight within one's moment-to-moment life, through awareness of one's patterns of diet, sleep, work-life balance, and other self-care. Some healers also engaged the client's cognitive understanding of the therapeutic process so that clients could consciously process and work with emotions, sensations, relational patterns, and whatever else may come up in the course of the treatment. The client's understanding supported the synergistic alignment of somatic and cognitive intelligence towards the attainment of a positive outcome. And as we have discussed earlier, healers prescribed specific meditative practices, when culturally appropriate, to bring the client's spirit into a state of healing.

# Part II

# Healers' Stories in Relation to Their Work

# Chapter 9

# Healer's Vision (Lama Jinpa)

One of the core questions with which I began this research is, does the way that the healer holds a vision of wholeness for the client, by consistently seeing the wholeness within, help anchor that experience of healing for people and communities?

The answer was, *undoubtedly, yes.* The healer must hold space for the client in this way; this supports the healing process. As healer Devatara Holman noted:

> First of all, the client must understand their own goodness, because a good deal of their suffering comes from not recognizing this goodness, their own true nature. That's where all of our suffering comes from. So, I establish with the patient that I recognize their primordial purity. And they need to recognize that also. The reason they are suffering is that they do not recognize that themselves and therefore feel separated. I recognize their primordial purity and by virtue of seeing that, it already grows. That establishes the ground of our relationship. They know that I am always looking at their best part. That's the center for a positive relationship, when they know that. And it also creates—it's a two-way thing. They must then look for that in me, as well.

And here is a second perspective, offered by Lama Jinpa:

> The vision of the healer—or the awareness of the healer— the knowledge, and that vision is informed by their perception of the individual: an accurate perception of the individual that, of course, the individual doesn't have about themselves. They don't see their wholeness particularly.

Much of my work is empowering another by being able to perceive what their true powerful nature is, or their true healthy nature is, underneath the veil. So one can see, even in spite of the relative rigidity of this formation, there are many different possibilities: particularly, the possibility of living as an accurate reflection of what you bring in; or, that accurate reflection being blocked in various ways. As far as the healer's consciousness goes, the minute someone steps into the room, for me, the healing is taking place because I am always seeing them in the most positive, i.e. accurate light. When I say *positive*, I don't mean positive thinking but that I am accurately perceiving their wholeness. That immediately has an inductive effect on them. It is inducing the possibility of them not only perceiving that, but starting to function [from that place]...If someone encourages you, believes in you, when no one else did before—it gives you a whole new perspective. When the healer is doing that on a subconscious level, on an awareness level, they're giving— they're empowering, literally, or initiating the person in such a way that it emboldens them to start living their real life— instead of a limited, karmically restricted life. That's a huge factor. That can be reinforced herbally, and reinforced by knowledge and information, and different things.

This understanding has implications for the way that we practice integrative medicine and counseling. In particular, this aligns with current research on developmental trauma disorders. We have seen that interpersonal traumatization, through neglect and other deficiencies in the development of healthy relational attachment, causes individuals to believe that they are flawed. The resultant chronic post-traumatic stress disorder (PTSD) has persistent effects on physical health, as well as psychosocial wellbeing. Further research should be done, using traditional Buddhist healing practices, to explore the effectiveness of these practices in treating developmental trauma disorders and the constellation of physical conditions linked to this diagnosis.

# Chapter 10

# Buddhist Medicine, American Culture: Healers' Cultural Adaptations to Diverse Client Communities

In Buddhist cultures, healers can freely prescribe a range of meditation practices and rituals, in the knowledge that their clients share their spiritual worldview. However, in the West even Tibetan doctors who are closely connected to the émigré community have very culturally and spiritually diverse clienteles: Most of their patients are not Buddhist. Accordingly, in keeping with the doctrine of *upaya* (skillful means), healers adapted their methods to align with the client's situation. Healers' cultural adaptations to the diversity of their client communities took four forms. First, they taught secular mindfulness meditation. Dr. Wangmo used mindfulness meditation with clients as a way of healing the physical and mental bodies simultaneously.

> Sometimes I am sitting with a patient who is taking herbs with me and say to them, maybe you can sit this way, and then breathing. Because you don't have to be Buddhist. Also: there is not any side effect. So this way, I sit with them and help them together, to show them how to do [meditation] together, to breathe, to stretch, certain things.

Second, they adjusted their conversation about diet and other lifestyle changes to the client's worldview. Dr. Smith described his practice of counseling a culturally diverse clientele:

> If I have a Hindu client or a yoga practitioner, I want to explain to them the three humors and the three doshas in a concrete way so that they can relate to their spiritual practice.

I'm not going to spend any time talking to them about Buddhism. ...So it really depends on who is in front of me. If a Christian comes in front of me I am not going to tell him that the reason why they're suffering in samsara is because they have a mistaken view of self. I won't even discuss it. It's not relevant to them. They need to meet it from their own spiritual tradition. So at that point, I will just explain as best I can, our concept of the three humors based upon the five elements in their body and how those three humors are made up out of the five elements. And how we work with medicine and diet and behavior and so forth, so that they can have the health outcome that they want.

A third adaptation was to keep the traditional practices intact within the healer's inner experience, while presenting the healing modality in a secular way. While working with their diverse clientele, eight of the healers performed mantra, visualizations and/or other rituals internally to support the healing work.

Juniper Foundation, a healing center, demonstrated a fourth adaptation: moving into a completely secular identity and healing approach while retaining the power of Tibetan Tantric healing lineages and Medicine Buddha practices. In the words of healer Christina Juskiewicz, Jupiter Foundation "has been working for over ten years to make the Buddhist path more accessible to a Western mind." The adaptations that Juniper Foundation has made are very comprehensive. In contrast to the maroon color that is characteristic of Tibetan cultural centers, the Juniper Foundation is furnished with a taupe waiting room, and treatment rooms are furnished with simple clinical beds. However, all clinicians have a commitment to do Medicine Buddha practice on a daily basis. When working with clients, they evoke this energy to create an energetic healing field through their own internal spiritual practice. Christina Juskiewicz described the secular visualization that is the client's work during a healing session.

> We have them focused on a blue light in their heart center. The blue light at their heart center has a very calming and grounding effect. This helps them to be more present, grounded and centered. And then we have them focus on a really deep sense of peace and harmony, tranquility and lovingkindness...This helps them reset: disengage from the world and reset their own feeling about themselves. It helps them to relax and be more receptive to the energy.

This visualization of a blue light at the heart's center is supported by the blue light cast by lamps in the treatment rooms. This visualization is very similar to the keynote of the traditional Medicine Buddha Puja, in which the Medicine Buddha, which symbolically embodies the qualities of peace, harmony, lovingkindness and stabilization, dissolves inside the practitioner's heart. Alternately, if the client is a meditation practitioner, the healer may have them envision the Medicine Buddha at their heart center. In this way, the client is receiving the benefit of this traditional practice that reconnects practitioners with an awareness of their own capacity for clarity, compassion, and peace, in a format that is accessible regardless of their spiritual affiliation or cultural background. All four of these adaptive paths represent creative solutions to the challenge of incorporating traditional Buddhist healing practices to the culturally diverse clientele found in the West.

# Part III

# Making the Connections:
# Consciousness and Healing

# Chapter 11

# How Does It Work? Paticca Samupadda

All healers spoke of *paticca samupadda*, or cause-and-effect, as a primary principle in their understanding of the causes of illness and wellness. Through their understanding of cause-and-effect, they were able to discern the root of a client's illness or imbalance. The healer established a relational ground with the client. Through this trustworthy relationship, the healer was then able to educate the client about the contributing causes of health and wellness, through which the client could then make appropriate changes in his or her self-care, relationships, and lifestyle. Additionally, the healer was able to use traditional healing rituals to bring about the intended result of physical, emotional, and spiritual balance. Within the range of Buddhist lineages represented in this study, this central theme emerged with a few variations. In healers' narratives, *paticca samupadda* discourse was often embedded within descriptions of five-elements theory and related practices of astrology. Five-elements theory and astrology praxis are expressions of Buddhist traditional healers' understanding of the law of cause-and-effect, or interdependence. The core insight that underlies these theories and practices is an understanding that there is ultimately no separation between the person and their environment, the pulses of the body, and the rhythms of the natural world.

Within Tibetan and Buddhist culture and medical theory, the implications of cause-and-effect are thus considered to extend beyond what logic can grasp. These implications are expressed in healers' narratives through their stories about the use of five-elements theory and astrology. Healers cited the centuries of empirical knowledge that are embedded within this approach as validation of their worldview. However, healers' interpretations

127

of the tenet of cause-and-effect varied. We can describe these variations with the terms tendrel, logic, subtle energies, and karma.

## Tendrel

*Tendrel* is the Tibetan translation of *paticca samupadda*; it bears the additional connotation of auspiciousness (Nalanda Translation Committee, 2003). Dr. Wangmo cited her personal experience with the practices of tendrel: "Personally I have had quite a strong tradition so I do follow, I do believe and then it does work." The experience of interdependence is dynamic, always emerging through interaction with the phenomenal world: To cite Geshe Chaphur, "we are just playing in the elements' playground." Within Tibetan and Buddhist culture and medical theory, the implications of cause-and-effect are thus considered to extend beyond what logic can grasp. Lama Jinpa described this traditional interpretation of tendrel:

> There are two ways one can be. One can perceive the world as a logical, rational, sequential, situation. But there is another way of perceiving it, or another way of starting to be, which is where things happen through tendrel, through connection. And they don't have logic. ...Whatever comes into the room is part of the story of the patient. Whether it's that they came late or when they were here it started raining. That's what I say about magical living: the more you are open to that, the more it happens, as we know.

## Logic

Within some Tibetan schools of thought, tendrel is parsed in psychological terms; within two healers' narratives, tendrel discourse can be tracked through the theme of logic. Venerable Thubten described this view of cause-and-effect:

We have a different kind of understanding of how that magic is working. It is working by psychological cause-and-effect. It is working because all these magical things you are looking at are creating impressions on the mind.

These impressions turned the mind towards self-reflective insight, which then brought about spiritual and possibly also physical healing. Within the healers' narratives, this view was countered by Lama Jinpa's description of tendrel as a process that operated outside of logic.

I tell people, there are two ways one can be. One can perceive the world as a logical, rational, sequential, situation. But there is another way of perceiving it, or another way of starting to be, which is where things happen through tendrel, through connection. And they don't have logic.

However, near the close of the interview with Venerable Thubten, when asked whether there was anything essential we had not discussed, she spoke of the field of blessing generated by the presence of an awakened being. That field of blessing reflected back the luminous awareness within hospice patients who received it, resulting in an extension of their lifespan and a state of psychospiritual integration, evidenced by (a) their sudden joy, and (b) the marked transformation of their intimate relationships towards a state of mutual engagement and growth in connection. The easiest way to understand these differences is as different points within the spectrum of Buddhist worldviews—there is a modern, scientific approach to traditional beliefs that is nonetheless mediated by traditional interpretations of tendrel. Dr. Holman described the benefit of this "third way": psychologically termed descriptions of cause-and-effect allay clients' concerns. At the same time, these traditional healers recognized the limits of established science, especially with regard to recognition and assessment of the subtle-energetic relational field created through practitioner-client intersubjectivity.

## Subtle Energies

In healers' accounts, subtle energies provided a vehicle through which intention and dependent arising produced psychospiritual and physical wellbeing. Lama Jinpa described these processes to his clients through the paradigm of energy medicine, which has been popularized by Larry Dossey and others. While Lama Jinpa's interpretation of his healing work was rooted in Buddhist teaching (including teaching on the three kayas and tendrel), he considered the language of bioenergetics more accessible to his clientele. Several healers were familiar with contemporary research in the field of energy medicine, and evinced hope that modern science would eventually support the empirical findings gleaned through their experience in the field.

Several healers described the causal vehicle of energy healing as interwoven with, or dependent on, the healer's positive energetic potential (alternately described as merit). Lama Tenzin Sherpa described this mechanism: "If the healer has peace of mind, energy flows very rapidly. A peaceful mind has a wider aura than an unpeaceful mind. So this is what helps us." Lama Tenzin's statement was in close concordance with Geshe Chaphur's description of healing work, which emphasized the primacy of "inner making space" in the development of healing potential. In Venerable Thubten's narrative, the positive potential within the energetic field of an enlightened teacher was able to effect spiritual and physical healing outside of a formal healing protocol: Intention and tendrel were sufficient. Within their framework, the healer's efficacy is achieved through nongrasping; this clears the healer's psychic space, so that the healer can be a conduit for subtle energies.

Healers who were trained in classical Chinese medicine,

Tibetan medicine, and Bon practice referenced the subtle channels as conduits for the movement of subtle energy. Two practitioners referenced Tsa-lung (Tibetan breath-yoga) as a regular meditation practice to balance their own body and mind. Tsa-lung practice harnessed the breath and intention to realign the subtle channels that together comprise an energetic anatomy interdependent with the physical body, so that consciousness and the physical body returned to a natural state of clarity, stability, and wellbeing.

Within Tibetan and Chinese acupuncture, the acupuncture meridians were used to move *chi*, vital energy, which then effected changes in physical wellbeing as well as changes in consciousness. While acupuncture is commonly practiced to bring about physical change, Buddhist traditional healers used this technique to bring about spiritual healing as well. Dr. Harding described a spiritual intervention case study:

> If someone's pulses indicate that the mind is not stable, that the mind is somehow separate from the body, it really is like a soul retrieval practice—from a classical Chinese medical point of view. The treatment I would do is working with the transporting points that are along the spine. Those points circulate the energetics of the elements and the organs. The treatment is about circulating what we call the "authentic chi" of those source points. The source of the water, the source of the fire—all of the elements. In that sense it is very much like a soul retrieval.

Within her Bon Buddhist practice, which has the closest alignment with shamanism of any Buddhist lineage, soul retrieval rituals reflect the wider ramifications of tendrel: a living connection with "universal energy" through the five elements and the natural world, which may need to be brought back into balance. This actively relational ontology shaped her work as a traditional

Buddhist practitioner, and imparted a greater symbolic density and transformative potential to the healing ritual of acupuncture. Lama Tenzin Sherpa, in his work, linked reiki healing with Buddhist mantra and mindfulness practice. While on certain occasions Lama Tenzin Sherpa drew on reiki symbols as a means to channel energy, and on other occasions, he simply sent energy through his hands, he did not differentiate between these healing energies and the increased energy that came through meditation practice. "It is for healing everything. ...It is for physical, emotional, mental, and spiritual levels. It works on all four levels." The healing ritual was shaped by his intention and attention, and assigned meaning through the relational ontology of *paticca samupadda*.

> There must be cause. What is the cause of problems? Maybe environment, maybe food, maybe family, maybe lack of peace, lack of rest, lack of exercise, maybe past life karma, or this life karma—some reason. I try to find all these things. Not only healing. Healing is just to provide energy, you know. I work through both levels—through the energy level and through Buddhist teaching, to find the causes.

## Karma

Within all of the healers' interpretations of cause-and-effect, karma (one's past actions) was described as a contributing factor within the etiology of illness and wellness. Dr. Holman shared with the researcher a phrasing of the Four Noble Truths (core Buddhist tenets) that she uses with clients to describe the role of karma.

> The first of those Four Noble Truths is that my suffering is the result of my negative thinking, negative karma and of course, my negative thinking and negative karma is the cause of my suffering and the condition for all sentient beings'

suffering. My happiness is the result of my positive thinking and positive karma—and my positive thinking and positive karma are the cause of my happiness and the condition for all sentient beings' happiness.

Self-grasping (through the misidentification of the self with one's thought patterns) was a contributing "distant cause" of spiritual and physical imbalance. Accordingly, Lama Tenzin Sherpa described the "near cause" of illness as the self-centered actions (karma) that arise from this mistaken view. Venerable Thubten, in her acknowledgement of the primary role of karma in medical and spiritual etiology, described the need to take direct action to bring about the change in karma that would effect a positive healing outcome: "Don't try, just do it." For this reason, rituals have been considered to be especially effective in the transformation of illness, in that they provide a skillful means to "counteract action with action" (Vargas, 2003, p. 121).

Lama Jinpa and other traditional healers applied a different nuance of expression within the discourse on karma: This misidentification with one's thoughts limited one's capacity to accurately perceive one's own wholeness. Due to the interdependence of body and mind, this mistaken view had implications for one's health. As Dr. Holman pointed out, "The body is just a reflection of the mind: It is the accumulation of our thinking. So, it reflects our thinking." Therefore, to change the body, one begins by changing the mind. These rituals worked on both mental and physical levels to effect the creation of health.

## The Field of Blessing (Venerable Thubten)

One healer, whose narrative had focused on the psychological aspects of Buddhist healing, completed her narrative with a story about the field of blessing generated by the presence of an enlightened teacher. She had witnessed several situations in which the blessing of a highly realized teacher effected both spiritual and physical healing. One client had arrived at their center with a back tumor, and a two-month prognosis. He wished to see the guiding teacher of the center. However, these meetings were exceedingly rare, and difficult to arrange. At that moment, the healer glanced out the window, and saw the guiding teacher: she responded, "It is your lucky day! We are going to go get a blessing." She then took the client to the guiding teacher, and described his situation. The teacher recited mantras over the client's body, and provided counsel for working consciously with death. Following this blessing, the client felt great joy and renewed energy; he lived for six more years.

On another occasion, a hospice patient was brought by a caregiver to the attention of three visiting teachers, who each recited mantras and bestowed their blessings upon him. He then recovered sufficiently from his illness to return to the east coast, to live with his sister for seven "very good" months.

# Chapter 12

# The Healer's Body as Initiation

A fourth view of *paticca samupadda* emerged from healers' narratives: the interdependence of the self and the physical world through the body of the healer. Within these narratives, it was clear that the healers' own embodied awareness—their own mind/body unity—was itself a vehicle for healing. In the West, we often refer to this as the paradigm of the "wounded healer." Several of these healers referenced the successful resolution of their own healing crises as the catalyst for their own healing praxis. As this study has noted, the language of illness and wellness has been used since the time of the Buddha to denote the path from misperception to realization.

This theme of the healer's journey as a microcosm of the collective healing journey is found throughout the Buddhist Canon. Vargas' (2003) study of illness and healing within the Tibetan *Dge slong ma Dpal mo* tradition discussed transformative healing crises within Buddhist narrative. Vargas stated that, within Buddhism, "illness appeared as an essential component of a practitioner's religious development or one of an enlightened being's tools for teaching" (p. 58). The renowned Tibetan master Milarepa is said to have worn illness as an ornament; Milarepa's clear perception of the true nature of illness and complete openness to this phenomenon prepared the ground for his practice of *tonglen*, sending blessing and receiving suffering (Vargas, 2003). Nun Gelongma Palmo, the revered practitioner who originated the Tibetan Nyung Nye ritual of fasting retreats, was tested in her meditation practice by the development of leprosy, triggered by the arising of karmic patterns from a past life. As Gelongma Palmo's leprosy increased, she practiced more deeply until her entire body was an open sore. At the point of death, Gelongma Palmo experienced a dream of being bathed in water. She woke up to find herself completely healed, the body restored to perfect wholeness. As Gelongma Palmo practiced with renewed faith and vitality, she attained realization and received the transmission of the Nyung Nye ritual directly from the Bodhisattva Avalokitesvara (Vargas, 2003).

The practitioners in this study who reported the experience of healing crises discussed the catalytic effect of their illnesses. Co-researcher Lama Tenzin Sherpa, having found himself near death and among the dying in a Nepal hospital, came to a deeper realization of the impermanence of life, the preciousness of human life, and the universality of suffering. This insight strengthened his vocation as a monk. The resolution of his illness through the energetic ministration of his teacher spurred Lama Tenzin Sherpa to extend his direction of service through the praxis of energetic healing.

Co-researcher Christina Juskiewicz experienced an energetic imbalance during a period of intensive meditation practice that exhausted her physical body and made it difficult to function. Her consultation with a range of Western and Ayurvedic physicians, while unsuccessful, ultimately led her to Segyu Rinpoche, who successfully cured her illness. Christina then studied with Segyu Rinpoche, holder of the Segyu lineage of Tibetan energetic healing, and went on to become a co-founder of Juniper Foundation, the healing institute associated with his work.

Co-researcher/acupuncturist Heidi Harding also began her path as a healer through serious illness. She had asthma and a chronic skin rash. Her perception of Western medical etiology was that its explanation of the causes and conditions of illness was incomplete: She sensed there was a greater contribution she could make to her own healing. Upon visiting an acupuncturist, Heidi experienced a full recovery and also was given meditation instruction. This experience spurred Heidi to study Bon meditation and the practice of acupuncture. Co-researchers Devatara Holman, Lama Jinpa, and Dr. Duran also alluded to catalytic processes of healing crisis that have informed their work. Their skillful use of self-as-instrument provides an empathic and embodied awareness of the healing journey that supports their cognitive understanding of healing praxis, in alignment with the principle of *paticca samupadda*, interdependent arising.

## Spiritual Crisis as Healer's Initiation (Lama Jinpa)

I got to a place in the three-year retreat where you lose everything. You lose all belief, you lose all hope, you lose everything you were hanging onto—it's gone. Even then, the ground fell out and I kept falling for another year, beyond "beyond." So when I got to the bottom, there was no Buddhism. There was no "anything"-ism. But what I found there, I've kept with me ever since—which is that presence that is tangible, real, and undeniably true.

Eventually, at some point, you start being confident that after about 45 minutes, the answer will come. No matter what else I do, after 45 minutes, I've got it. So it's like that sense of confidence in reality, in Buddha nature: I have such confidence in the five elements, or the five wisdoms, and I have such confidence in consciousness, and I have such confidence in the brilliance of human beings, that I know. I absolutely know, whoever walks into the room, I will have the correct answer. That doesn't mean I will cure everything. But I have absolute confidence that I will accurately perceive.

Lama Jinpa's case illustrates the common pattern of the "breakdown to break through" which is found in the lineage stories of many Buddhist teachers and healers. On the path to diamond-point clarity, the initiate is tested by fire, which clarifies confusion. Body and mind both serve as the instruments through which experiences of pain catalyze the transformative journey of the initiate, and ultimately open the door to their path of service.

## Chapter 13

# Paticca Samupadda and the New Neuroscience

Now that we have seen how deeply the healing work, as described by these veteran healers, rests upon *paticca samupadda*, let's look at some modern scientific paradigms that help to provide context, to translate the poetry of these traditional healing practices into the precision of science. First of all, the emergent field of interpersonal neurology offers a strong reference point, one that is cited by our healers, to describe the healing efficacy of their practices.

## Interpersonal Neuropsychological Research and the Element of Space

Venerable Thubten described the healing efficacy of the Medicine Buddha Puja by citing leading-edge neuropsychological research on empathy and attunement. This neuropsychological model also provides useful contextualization in the related narrative of her hospice caregiving, which, as she noted, challenged us to develop a new definition of healing.

Current research in interpersonal neuropsychology has charted the benefits of mindful therapeutic presence, empathy, and attunement through studies of the psychological phenomenon of secure attachment. Within a Tibetan Buddhist context, mindful therapeutic presence, empathy, and attunement are described through the theme of space. There is a very close connection between the neuropsychological discourse on secure attachment and the Buddhist Five Element discourse on space. This point of correlation is currently being investigated by neuroscientists and Buddhist practitioners alike, with tremendous curiosity and interest. Here, we will explore the healers' understandings of the element of space and then discuss its neurological correlation with regard to the processes of secure attachment. This will help to illuminate a few of the causal pathways, traditionally described as *paticca samupadda*, that support traditional Buddhist healing.

## Space

As discussed earlier, the element of space carries several different levels of meaning for Buddhist practitioners. Within Five Element theory, the element of space represents consciousness. The mind is considered to be as vast and clear as the open sky. In order to prepare for their work with clients, healers engaged in mindfulness practice. Mindfulness was an act of "inner making space," in the words of Geshe Chaphur, that made it possible for healers to be unconditionally present to their own experience.

This quality of "inner making space" has a parallel in modern psychology—the state of *unintegration*, first identified by the psychoanalyst Donald Winicott (Epstein, 1999, p. 36): a space of being rather than doing. This state of unintegration takes place within an inner *holding environment*, a nurturing sense of self-containment, similar to that space that a wise parent provides for their child, present without interfering. Within a state of unintegration, a person is present to themselves with "unrestricted, unimpaired awareness" (Epstein, 1999, pp. 36–7). In healers' work, this capacity for "inner making space," or unintegration, made it possible for the healers to create sacred space for their work, both physically and psychically. Through this ritual of creating space within, the healer was then able to offer the client a wide and open relational field (analogous to the holding environment Winicott described). In the words of Heidi Harding:

We are...creating an open space, where people can allow themselves to be seen. I think a lot of the work is just bearing witness to people's experiences, people's pain. Creating an openness—just that openness in the sacred space together—is very powerful.

As mentioned earlier in Chapter 5, the healer's ritual of mindfulness, a creating of space for his- or herself, and the ritual of creating space for the client were different facets of one practice. Through interpersonal resonance, this quality of "stillness, silence, and spaciousness" (per Heidi Harding), as embodied by the healer, gave the client the opportunity to realign his or her body-mind to this place of wholeness and balance. Thus, in the healer's work, the ritual of creating space prepared the ground for the ritual of therapeutic attunement. To cite co-researcher Heidi Harding, "That interplay between patient and practitioner, between heart and mind, for both of us—is the first treatment, the first way of moving chi." This interplay is a vehicle for healing: As Devatara Holman noted, when the therapeutic relationship is strengthened, the patient discovers their capacity for healing relationships in every aspect of life.

This understanding is increasingly congruent with psychology, as the field of psychology itself evolves, and incorporates knowledge gleaned through contemplative practices, and confirmed by science. Within counseling psychology, it is also understood that the capacity to create a holding environment for oneself and enter into a state of unintegration is a prerequisite to the creation of a holding environment for the client—in which they can be with their own experiences (Epstein, 1999). By extending this spaciousness to themselves, good therapists are then well equipped to extend the spaciousness of deep listening to their clients.

## Meditation, Healing, and Healthy Attachment

Within humanistic psychology, the healing potential of the

therapeutic relationship is understood through the lens of secure attachment, an idea that has long been associated with the process of children's emotional development, and now is seen to have increasing relevance in all human relationships. While, as a practitioner, I don't believe that every aspect of meditation can be mapped by bioscience, it certainly provides a useful lens in discussions of Buddhist healing. I am reminded of the Buddha's parable of the raft, in which the wise person uses the raft to cross a wide river, then releases it once the crossing is accomplished. In the same way, we can use psychobiology as a skillful means to reconcile the traditional and modern aspects of this dialogue. So, let's consider the scholarship.

The effect of meditation upon anxiety and other afflictive emotions has now been well documented by Jon Kabat-Zinn,[1] Herbert Benson,[2] and many others. The effect of meditation upon the physical body is also now quite well understood through the mechanism of the parasympathetic nervous system, which evokes the relaxation response. There are additional direct connections between emotional and physical resiliency, through the neuropsychology of secure attachment, which we will explore in this chapter.

The new findings in the field of interpersonal neurology are most significant because they are changing our paradigms of bioscience. The paradigms we adopt have implications for the way we live our lives. Physics, as a science, has been more flexible in its adaptation of new models of reality. In the Newtonian period, it posited a world of separate atoms as the building blocks of all reality. This translated, in the human sciences, to a social Darwinism, upheld by atomistic concepts of the self.[3] There is a natural sequence, a "trickle-down" relationship, connecting our ontology to epistemology to praxis to ethics.[4] As we have moved to a greater awareness of systems and interconnection in physics, and of the ecology of living systems in biology, so our models of the human body are also undergoing change.

Classically, the response of the central nervous system (CNS) was understood as hierarchical—sensory input arises from the body to the brain. The brain then governs the body's response. Now that process is understood as more bidirectional—the brain is getting information from the limbic system. The more integrated that flow of energy and information, the greater one's capacity for emotional and physical health. Within the prior biological model, the mind was understood simply as a function of the brain. Psychiatrist Daniel Siegel, whose interpersonal neuropsychological research has enhanced our understanding of the connections between meditation and health, defines the mind as "an embodied and relational emergent process that regulates the flow of energy and information."[5] This paradigm change is important. As I have mentioned earlier, these paradigms do affect our ethics, and our way of being in the world. If the mind is only in the brain, the implications are that we do not have to see our interdependence with the world. We can treat it as an object whose ultimate end does not concern us too much, and we will inevitably also objectify people. On the other hand, when we adopt this "embodied" and "relational emergent" definition of the mind, we are already shifting our understanding towards an interdependent and relational ethics, which is true to the connected nature of reality itself.

Contemporary research in interpersonal neurology shows us that the mind is throughout the body—the limbic system, the heart, the brain are in a dialogue that is truly bidirectional. Dr. Siegel and other neuropsychology pioneers have well described the correlations between the strength of this bidirectional process, the relational patterns in early life, our way of being with ourselves, and our relationship to the world around us. To more deeply understand this, we will now visit the neuropsychology involved in the formation of healthy relationships.

## I. Introduction to Attachment Theory

Current research has shown a deep connection between secure attachment, resiliency, and meditation. This provides insight into the role of meditation in the achievement of integration, a cornerstone of health.

Attachment, within psychology, is defined as "the lasting psychological connectedness between human beings."[6] Secure attachment is the foundation for healthy relationships. The capacity for trust, openness, and flexibility in connection with others begins with our first relationships: our parents or primary caregivers. During the first two years of life, the brain is still forming; its capacity for integration is directly impacted by this relational experience with our parents. This capacity for integration is directly related to our capacity for emotional self-regulation, and these primary relationships serve as a template for all our intimate relationships.[7]

From the very beginning of our life, we are already interdependent with other people. Before a baby has even opened its eyes, it already has experienced its interdependence through its mother's milk. Shortly after birth, it recognizes its mother's face, and can pick up minute changes in her expression as it attunes to her emotional state.[8] These are the earliest stirrings of our natural drive towards connection. Psychologist John Bowlby, the founder of attachment theory, theorized that through the fulfillment of this drive, a parent-child bond is established that provides the baby with physical safety.[9] Subsequent research has proven his theorem that healthy attachment is not only a physical necessity, but also fundamental to our growth in relationship.[10] Through the parent's awareness of the child, and accurate mirroring of its feelings and being, the child experiences a core experience of attunement that supports healthy connection and also honors the differentiation of a secure sense of self.[11] That sense of attunement and mutuality is at the heart of all human relationships. This relationship also literally shapes the brain, as we will explore next.

## II. Interpersonal Neuropsychology

Research has brought us a deeper understanding of the effects of healthy attachment by tracking the neurological pathways related to the inner process of attachment. This has provided insight into the way that meditation heals by catalyzing mind-body integration, and fostering the development of "earned" secure attachment in later life.

The brainstem, limbic region, and neocortex, taken together, form the "triune brain." These three layers of the brain developed at different stages of the evolutionary journey, and thus there is a marked differentiation with regard to their functions. The brainstem is the first layer; it is a very simple level of function that we share with fish and reptiles. The brainstem regulates autonomic nervous system processes, such as digestion, breathing, and heartbeat, as well as shaping the energy level of the upper levels (limbic system and neocortex). It also conveys energy and information from the central nervous system (throughout the body) to the upper regions of the brain.

The limbic system is the middle layer of the triune brain, a region we share with all mammals. The limbic system provides us with the capacity for emotion—this is a useful evolutionary function, as emotion is essentially an assessment of value that leads us to take action. Additionally, the amygdala stores memories in an implicit (unconscious) form. Its memory storage is primed towards memories that are visceral, and that have a strong charge. This begins before birth: Sensory input can already be shown to be registering in the womb, as well as the effects of maternal neurotransmitters and hormones. This is a right-hemispheric limbic process—and therefore emphasizes the emotional and somatic processes that are the right brain's domain. In the first few years of life, until the neocortex fully develops, this is the only memory system that is "online." After the first few years of life, the hippocampus (a memory-mapping system within the limbic system) and the prefrontal cortex develop and work together, to convert moment-by-moment experiences into memories, and to link discrete memories into narrative. When we're forming our attachment patterns, though, this is all we have. Therefore all our attachment patterns are based in right brain to right brain bodily-based experiences between parent and child that are drawn from implicit memory, and thus largely unconscious.[12]

In order for us to become aware of those feelings inside us—to work with them consciously—we need to link these limbic emotional states to our cortex. That linkage is referred to as *vertical integration*.

The neocortex was the last part of the brain to evolve. We share some of its functions with other mammals, and most of its functions with primates, whales and dolphins.[13] Deep inside the neocortex, there is a region, known as the insula cortex, that supports the flow of information between the brainstem, central nervous system, limbic system, and neocortex. The insula cortex not only conveys information about the state of the body; it also gathers this information into a meaningful context. The insula cortex receives signals from mirror neurons in the motor areas, anterior cingulate, and other areas of the cortex: These mirror neurons map the "sensory implications of motor actions."[14] The anterior insula's body-state awareness is constantly mediated by the middle prefrontal region of the cortex, and its capacity for self-awareness.

## A. Integration

As the brain develops into its full capacity, it becomes increasingly important that these various embodied processes of energy and information are well integrated. There are two kinds of integration: **horizontal integration** (right-left hemisphere integration, also known as bilateral integration) and **vertical integration** (body and limbic system with neocortex). While horizontal integration always takes the same pathway (through the corpus callasum), there are various paths through which the vertical integration can take place. This flow of energy and information helps integrate the somato-emotional intelligence of the right hemisphere with the reasoning of the left hemisphere, and allows us to relationally connect in an attuned, sensitive, and grounded way. This inner integration is the key to our self-insight, our relational health, and our experience of an interconnected world. This natural and deep correlation between sensory awareness, self-awareness, and empathy is described in Buddhism through the concept of rupa-skandas. In the words of a co-researcher:

> The rupa skanda is made up of ten things: it's made up of your five sense organs, and five sense objects. Right now, you and I don't consider that we're sitting in the same room [we are on Skype]. But we're actually, at this moment, sharing the same rupa skanda, because we're both acting as visual and auditory objects of one another. It is profoundly nondual if you really understand what abhidharma's actually talking about. What they're saying is, if you go and strike somebody, you might be hitting someone else's body, but you're effectively doing violence to your own rupa skanda. So when I am treating a patient, I am not just treating a patient, I am also treating myself. That person—now they're in front of me—that means they're part of my rupa skanda. I'm part of their rupa skanda. This is where the language of self frays badly at the edges. (Dr. Malcolm Smith)

## B. Empathy

The integration we experience between the limbic system (body-based awareness) and the prefrontal cortex (via the anterior insula and mirror neurons) makes empathy possible. We experience empathy through the medium of our physical body. To understand the importance of integration more deeply, we will look at the mirror neurons, which provide the basis for empathy.

Through the activity of mirror neurons, and the consequent sensing of bodily states that arises in the prefrontal area by means of the insula cortex, we know another person's physical position; through this mirror neuron system, we also have the capacity to sense another's feelings in our own body. The mirror neuron system that registers our physical sensation is the same system that registers awareness of another's feeling.

As the information about another's feeling state is sent through our nervous system, it creates a physical response within us. Our heart rate changes, we feel physically relaxed, or we tighten up. This is valuable information: By listening to the physical cues presented by our own body, we can sense the appropriate social response.

That initial information is then sent from the insula cortex down through the body, where it is amplified by the HPA (hypothalamic-pituitary-adrenal) axis, releasing hormones that trigger a second level of psychophysical response so that the sensations are fully experienced. Empathy is thus the sum of these body and limbic shifts—our capacity to perceive and respond. This felt sense of empathy is then further refined by other mirror neurons that attribute this feeling either to ourselves or to another.

So, there is a deep learning process going on. By tuning into our own body, and our felt experience, we know and sense another's felt experience. Through knowing and sensing another person's felt experience, we are also made aware of another person's emotions. When we sense another's feelings in our own body, this is the core of empathy. The connection is happening through our body, but is truly a somato-emotional experience.

### III. Attachment Styles

As we have discussed earlier in this chapter, the capacity for this attunement to our bodies, our emotions, and the felt experience of another is hard-wired within our neurology—particularly in the first years of childhood. That primary experience of healthy relational attachment, the parent's awareness of the child, and accurate witnessing of its feelings and being provides the ground through which the child can experience inner freedom and security. This is commonly known as secure attachment. The psychologist D. W. Winicott emphasized the role of attachment security in the development of a private self. The parent's capacity to create a holding environment for the child—a wide and open, yet consistently present relational field—provides the child with the security it needs to attend to its own process. Out of this experience of having its emotional needs met, the child develops a basic trust in its felt experience: its emotions, its body, and the expression of psychological needs; with this, we can say that a sense of authenticity is developed. These are the characteristics of a *secure* attachment style. In adult life, secure attachment expresses itself through the capacity for true intimacy and clear communication with another person.

As Tolstoy once said, "Happy families are all alike. Every unhappy family is unhappy in its own way."[15] So it is that within psychology, there is just one model of secure attachment, and a few variations on insecure attachment.

Within insecure attachment, the needs for healthy relational attachment were not met: Specific deficiencies are catalogued into the three types of insecure attachment. Insecure attachment can be further classified as Dismissive/Avoidant, Preoccupied/ Ambivalent, or Disorganized.

Within the situation that psychology describes as **avoidant** attachment, one or both parents took a dismissive stance with regard to attachment: that is, when the child reached out with an emotional need, the parent discouraged it, in some way shut it down. The child then associated its attempts at closeness with pain. The parent-child dyad can be characterized as having a quality of rigidity. Out of this early experience, a defense mechanism developed that suppressed that urge towards connection, and capacity to feel resonance. These individuals live out of the logic-driven left brain, and do not consciously experience the full somato-emotional expression of the right brain. Given that the circuitry which gives us awareness of others' feelings is the same circuitry which gives us awareness of our somatic and emotional experience, these individuals may experience diminished connection with their bodies and diminished affective expression. However, without bilateral (right and left brain) integration, narrative and memory integration and fluid interpersonal presence are not possible. As an adult, this person may go on to experience depression, or persistent dissatisfaction with their close relationships, but typically would not have the emotional self-insight to discern the roots of their unhappiness.

Within the relationship pattern known as **ambivalent** attachment, the parent was emotionally present intermittently, but not attuned to the child. The parent may have been overwhelmed by anxiety or depression, or simply not skilled in creating the healthy bonding consistent with good parenthood. Out of the parent's lapses, the child's nervous system registers a sense of potential danger. However, with every moment of presence, the child's system registers the possibility of mirroring, warmth, and the fulfillment of his or her needs. This inconsistent reinforcement sets the child's sympathetic nervous system into sentinel mode: always on alert, chronically hyper-aroused. The containment and inner security associated with consistent parenting is absent—and therefore, there is a specific kind of integration that is absent. The neural pathways that connect the right limbic system with the middle prefrontal region contain spaces of disconnection. The right limbic neural nets that are not woven into connection with the prefrontal region are unstable. They may carry considerable somato-emotional energy, which suddenly disrupts the activity of our higher brain functions when triggered. The term "limbic lava" has been coined to describe this volatile somato-emotional energy that arises from the implicit memory process of the amygdala (Siegel, 2010). Due to these disassociated neural nets, and the resultant energy surges, the sense of self is not so coherent. The child's early anxiety may imprint within their system as an overactive right-brain system, periodically flooded by the overstimulated limbic system. The integrative need, in this case, is for the left-mode organization and containment that supports the assimilation of right-mode somato-emotional experiences.

There is a third, less prevalent insecure attachment style, known as **disorganized attachment**. In the case of disorganized attachment, the parents were so continually immersed in past experience, due to trauma or a preexistent mental health condition, that they were not able to provide safety for the child. Reinforcement of healthy vulnerability and connection is less consistent, and perhaps does not exist at all. The parent-child dyad is characterized by both chaos and rigidity. The child therefore lives in the implicit memory of the amygdala (rather than the explicit memory of the neocortex or integrated body-mind) since there is no opportunity for the amygdala to relax. For this child, their inner life is an experience of fear without a solution, and cognitive confusion.[16]

These attachment patterns, set within the first two years of life, serve as the template for all our significant relationships. Attachment security has been shown to correlate with greater adult emotional self-regulation, self-esteem, and self-agency.[17] Insecure attachment has been implicated as a risk factor in anxiety, depression, and other psychiatric disorders.[18] Attachment security has also been shown to facilitate the higher states of spiritual integration—the consciousness of ethics, morality, insight, creativity, and intuition.[19]

Further studies have shown a correlation between childhood

attachment states and adult health outcomes. A longitudinal study of children classified as insecure attached showed these individuals were more likely to develop inflammation-based illnesses in adulthood.[20] Although the Adverse Childhood Experiences (ACE) Study is not specifically concerned with attachment, it is a landmark study that incorporated many social markers of insecure attachment into its questionnaire design. In this study, the Centers for Disease Control (CDC) surveyed 17,000 adults, and found powerful correlations between childhood trauma and chronic disease, health risk behaviors, and reproductive health.[21] These findings, taken together, would suggest that, as a society, we have a vested interest in the reduction of attachment insecurity. Contemporary research shows that meditation promotes the achievement of "earned" secure attachment through several integrative processes.

## IV. Restoration of Healthy Attachment

Mindfulness meditation practices, such as those found within these Buddhist traditions, bring awareness to the body, and to the present moment. This has the effect of weaving disassociated limbic neural networks into connection with the prefrontal cortex. Through this vertical integration, the stored somato-emotional energy in the limbic system becomes less volatile, and the individual experiences a greater sense of safety. For the meditator who has an insecure ambivalent attachment history, this may have the effect of providing an inner containment and witnessing ascribed to the "good enough" parent who is optimally present, without interfering. For the meditator who has an insecure avoidant attachment history, this vertical integration supports the development of those right-hemispheric somato-emotional connections that were lacking in their early life. Through this, they may experience new seeds of vitality and zest within all their relationships. For adults with a history of disorganized attachment, trauma-specific approaches are sometimes necessary, to ensure that the individual's mind is not flooded with the raw emotional material that comes to the surface. Mindfulness-based cognitive therapy and dialectical behavioral therapy are among the mindfulness-based psychotherapeutic protocols that have been adapted for those in recovery from trauma.

However, even in these sensitive communities, meditation has been shown to bring about healing. This is because meditation helps us to see our story and to recognize that we are not that story. Through the practices of meditation, we integrate the limbic and cortical areas (and with them, the body and mind). We gain greater self-awareness and inner freedom. As a wise person once said, we "don't believe everything we think." (This capacity to step back, perceive the habitual stories of the mind, and disidentify with them, is the outcome of increased vertical and horizontal integration.) Through this shift in awareness, we can consciously choose how to write our story rather than being overwhelmed by unconscious material, or shut off from our physical body. This inner integration ultimately catalyzes growth in all those whose lives we touch.

Long-term meditators have thicker cortical layers than non-meditators; this cortical growth shows increased neuroplasticity (capacity to form new neural connections), as well as increased strength within existing synaptic connections. This difference is most pronounced in the right hemisphere, and within the insula cortex[22] — which, as we have seen, are critical areas with regard to healthy attachment: The thickened insula cortex provides greater capacity for empathy and self-insight.[23]

Thus the same mindfulness practice that strengthens our inner spaciousness, and personal integration, makes it possible for us to be with others in an attuned and empathic way. This quality of empathy, provided through the resonance circuitry, provides a sense of safety and containment that may have been lacking in the client's childhood. In the words of a co-researcher:

We are...creating an open space, where people can allow themselves to be seen. I think a lot of the work is just bearing witness to people's experiences, people's pain. Creating an openness — just that openness in the sacred space together — is very powerful. (Dr. Heidi Harding)

Four core elements of therapeutic attunement have been identified by neuropsychiatrist Daniel Siegel, which correlate with mindfulness practice and the therapeutic effect of Buddhist healers. These are *presence*, through which the therapist is open to the client unconditionally; *attunement*, which makes it possible for the therapist to listen to the client with the fullness of his or her kinesthetic awareness; *resonance*, the creation of a therapeutic dyad that is both emotionally and kinesthetically in close rapport; and *tracking*, the sum of these elements: the active whole-body listening to the energy and information flow within the therapeutic dyad, and the practice of communicating this flow in the "here-and-now" (Siegel, 2010b).

Tracking, in its primary quality of perception and response, is the practice of therapeutic empathy and integrative therapist-client process. It is also well embedded within traditional healing practices. Tracking can occur within the context of an intake interview; it can also take place on a somatic, experiential level with these traditional healing practices, including within the classical Chinese and traditional Tibetan practice of pulse-taking. The depth of mindfulness and relational attunement make it possible to discern the pulse with greater subtlety and precision.

While this quality of full awareness is characteristic of many therapeutic modalities, Siegel underscored the need for tracking awareness to be accompanied by unconditional acceptance and kindness; these affective qualities, within the felt experience of tracking, serve as the catalyst for a corrective emotional experience (Siegel, 2010b). The theme of compassion was central to the experience of our co-researchers, whose voices were in unanimity at this point: "the seed of the doctor is compassion." These neuropsychological processes serve as the physical foundation for experiences of empathy, trust, and emotional resonance reported by traditional Buddhist healers as cornerstones of their work. Through an examination of these current neuropsychology findings, it becomes apparent that the mindfulness practices of Buddhist healers support their "inner making space," and their capacity for creating a healing relationship with their clients, which then has both psychological and physical effects.

## Meditation and Physical Healing

There are many tangible physical benefits associated with meditation. The body-mind's habitual stress responses, mediated through the sympathetic nervous system, can cause chronic dysregulation that may include headaches, cardiac arrhythmia, digestive issues, backaches, sleep issues, anxiety, and depression. Chronic dysregulation is a compounding factor in many of the adverse health outcomes tracked through the ACE study. Through meditation we experience an activation of the parasympathetic nervous system: the renewal of full circulation to the internal organs, lowering blood pressure and heart rate, shifting the body back into homeostasis.

For a long time, the expression of our genetic inheritance was considered to be set in stone: From the moment we were conceived, the gene's expression was immutable. Now it is understood that gene expression connected to immune response, longevity, and other aspects of health is modified by neuropeptides, the molecules that convey our emotional response throughout the body—our genetic expression is adversely affected by stress, positively affected by yoga and meditation. The integrative healing work we do today thus affects not only ourselves, but generations to come. Our future as a society depends upon it.

## Tibetan Tantric Buddhist Rituals: Integration of Primal Energy

The Medicine Buddha Puja has a well-defined niche within a wide range of Mahayana Buddhist practices. Our healers attributed its efficacy both to psychological processes of resonance and to the sacred archetypal energy of the Medicine Buddha. Within these healers' narratives, the powerful rituals that are specific to Vajrayana (Tantric) Buddhism have also come to light. Within Vajrayana tradition, participation in many traditional rituals and personal practices is reserved for the initiated. This presented a research quandary, as the healing Chod ritual and Vajrasattva practices were central to the spoken and performed narratives of several Tibetan Buddhist co-researchers (as we have discussed in Chapter 4). As part of my fieldwork, I received the empowerment to perform Chod practice, and took up this practice with the local Tibetan Bon Buddhist community. This firsthand experience provided me with a clear sense of the synergistic effect of the use of melody, instruments, and text in producing the quintessential transformative power within Chod. Within this, the psychospiritual potency of working with primal emotions also became clear.

The Chod melody focuses the practitioner's somato-emotional energy to support the practitioner's archetypal journey to the ritual ground. The sounding of the *kangling* (ritual trumpet fashioned of human thigh bone), which begins the Chod ceremony, introduces the primal power of this ritual. The rhythm and tonal frequency of the bell and *damaru* (hand-drum) punctuate the Chod ritual, providing a kind of sonic driving that integrates the practitioner's core consciousness with the primal energy of the somato-emotional system. The audible elements of Chod ritual are combined with the internal activity of performing visualizations, so that, as Cupchik (2013) noted, "the total symbolic meaning of music is greater than the sum of all audible parts" (pp. 120–1). The somato-emotional intensity of Chod ritual is highly intentional in its harnessing of primal energy towards the healing outcome. This intentional practice of contacting and transmuting instinctual somato-emotional energy is the distinguishing attribute of Vajrayana (Tantric) Buddhism.

This alchemical process may be especially valuable in the healing process. Buddhist texts attribute the origin of illness to the three poisons: anger, desire, and ignorance (Birnbaum, 1979; Clifford, 2006; Zysk, 1991). Activity based on attachment and identification with these destructive emotions is considered to bring about illness and the full range of karmic causality (Birnbaum, 1979; Clifford, 2006; Zysk, 1991). However, repression of these instinctual energies is also detrimental to health, as the negative emotions may become somaticized (Preece, 2006). On the other hand, if these instinctual forces are consciously engaged, they can provide the means for physical and emotional health, and more deeply integrated spiritual development. Carl Jung (1968) described this conscious engagement of the archetypal as the proper function of symbol. In order to transform instinctual energy, the symbol needed to have charge and numinosity. Preece (2006) noted that the symbolic channel needed "to be of the same nature as the forces transformed" (p. 183): Working with energies of fear, fear is evoked; with energies of desire, desire is evoked. "The symbolic deity that will lift the Shadow into Consciousness must embody the wisdom that realizes the essential nature of the force to be transformed" (Preece, 2006, pp. 183–4). This experience of healing through work with the dark emotions was relayed through the healers' narratives of Chod practice. However, it was when I participated with the local Chod community that the distinctively Vajrayana elements of this healing ritual, and its symbolic power, became evident through direct experience. The psychotherapeutic potential within these techniques that Tibetan Buddhism has developed for reintegrating repressed or unintegrated elements of the psyche through the intentional activation of primal energies (through which contact with the original unintegrated material is made) and the subsequent re-entrainment of the limbic and cognitive consciousnesses would benefit from further study, particularly as there are parallels in current somato-emotional approaches to trauma recovery (Van der Kolk, 2015).

## Tibetan Buddhist Healing and Subtle Energy: Bioenergetic Research

Seven of the healers described their work in terms of the traditional three levels of Buddhist medicine: body, mind, and subtle energies. Two made reference to the concept of *lung*, energy-wind, which is used in traditional Tibetan Buddhist healing systems to describe the point of connection between consciousness and the physical body. The concept of *lung* is foreign to our Western paradigms—perhaps this is because, according to the Tibetan healers I surveyed, most Westerners could be diagnosed with *lung* imbalance.

The energy-wind, or subtle body, functions as an intermediary between the body and consciousness, translating intention from mind to body, and translating physical sensations from body to mind (Preece, 2006). (For more on this, see our description of Sambhogakaya in Chapter 2.) The Tibetan symbol that expresses the correspondence between consciousness and subtle energy is the *lunglu*, or windhorse. When the windhorse of subtle energy is wild and rough, consciousness will also be agitated; when the windhorse is refined and smooth, consciousness will be calm. Current scholarship suggests that the nervous system is analogous (although not identical) to the Tibetan medical understanding of *lung* (Dagpa & Dodson-Lavelle, 2009, p. 183). Tantric Tibetan Buddhist texts describe yogic practices through which attention and intention can be focused within these subtle-energy systems to effect physiological changes including changes in body temperature and respiration (Dalai Lama, 1991). Tsa-lung interventions practiced with lymphoma patients improved their quality of life, mood, sleep quality, physical functioning, and overall wellbeing (Chaoul, 2011). Research that has been done on Tibetan Buddhist Tsa-lung meditations and other subtle-channel healing paradigms (Benson, 1991; Chaoul, 2011; Chaoul-Reich, Cohen, Fouladi, Rodriguez, & Warneke, 2004) suggests that these traditional frameworks known as subtle channels incorporate a distinctive and potentially valuable resolution of the philosophical and scientific questions regarding the mind-body connection.

In a traditional Buddhist healing setting, the subtle channels of classical Chinese medicine and Tibetan medicine are understood to transfer the energy of the mind via intention into the physical body. The classical Chinese acupuncture subtle channels of *Ren Mai*, *Du Mai*, and *Chong Mai* are considered to correspond to the three subtle channels of Tibetan medicine. Through *Tsa-lung* practices, a patient can treat and access these channels within themselves (co-researcher Harding, 2014). Further research in this area could help clarify the role of these subtle channels in effecting mind-body integrative health.

The empirical research to support this understanding may be forthcoming. Methods for measuring subtle energy are becoming more refined. In a related study of energy healing, individuals have been found to exchange cardiac energy when in proximity; this energetic exchange is more pronounced when an individual's electromagnetic field is brought into coherence through thoughts of love or caring (Atkinson, McCraty, Tiller, & Tomasino, 1998). A meta-analysis of distant intentionality and healing studies showed robust and replicable effect sizes across experiments (Braud & Schlitz, 1997). This finding poses a challenge for the biological sciences, in that consciousness, in these experiments, is identified as causal. Classical Chinese acupuncture meridian points have been found to have unique electroconductive properties (Voll, 1975). As magnetic field measurements of bioenergy become increasingly subtle, there is the potential that both classical Chinese and Tibetan subtle channels used in traditional Buddhist healing will be identified as a bridge between consciousness and matter—one that utilizes particularly electroconductive channels to convey the intentionality and cardiac energy from healer to client.

## Core Components of the Healing Process across Cultures

While this study focused upon Buddhist healers across cultures, the participation of a co-researcher who identifies as Native American and works actively as a healer within diverse Indigenous societies brought the researcher to actively question whether there are core ritual components of the healing process that can be identified across traditional cultures. Both Buddhist and indigenous cultures frame reality in the context of relationships (Wilson, 2008). As noted earlier, dialogic interaction between Tibetan Buddhism and indigenous Bon practices has gone on for centuries, transforming both traditions. Tibetan spirituality, suffused with both traditions, lifts up an ecological vision of interrelationship—through which individual relationships, brought into reciprocity, create a world in harmony (Abram, 1996; Macy, 1978; Snyder, 2000; Sumegi, 2008).

Therefore, we can look to convergences in practices and findings within indigenous and transcultural scholarship, that may illuminate the core elements of healing ritual. The anthropologist Joan Koss-Chioino conducted field research in Puerto Rico and Latin American countries on Indigenous spirituality and healing. Koss-Chioino then collaborated in the interdisciplinary STRP (Spiritual Transformation Scientific Research Program), which sought to identify universal factors that influence the process of spiritual transformation (Metanexus Institute, 2004). Based on this research, Koss-Chioino (2006a) hypothesized a global model of healing ritual—one in which the particularities of mythic mapping, symbology, and ritual tools were more about content than foundational process, which could be seen to be congruent, not only across cultures, but within both spiritual and psychotherapeutic modalities.

Koss-Chioino's model centered upon three components: transformation, relation, and *radical empathy*, a state in which the healer's and client's experiences are felt by the healer as a single relational field (Koss-Chioino, 2006b). This concept of radical empathy is analogous to psychoneurologist Dan Siegel's concept of integrative *joining*: Through tracking, the therapist's whole-body listening and attunement to the client, accompanied by unconditional acceptance and kindness, a level of resonance is achieved that catalyzes the therapist's interoceptive awareness of a connection "before and beyond words" (Siegel, 2010b, p. 142). Koss-Chioino's discovery of the centrality of radical empathy to the healing process is congruent with the narratives of our traditional Buddhist healers: In the words of co-researcher Dr. Wangmo, "the seed of the doctor is compassion."

Koss-Chioino focused on the healing journey as a spiritual transformation—a life passage that brought about "dramatic changes in world and self views, purposes, religious beliefs, attitudes or behaviors" (Katz, 2004, p .15). She also described the phenomenon of the "wounded healer," the initiation of the healer through their own successful resolution of somato-emotional and spiritual healing crises, which we have discussed here. As our healers noted, there needs to be a *change of consciousness* in order for healing to take root. In our explorations of healing ritual, spiritual transformation is identified with the rituals of *evoking sacred power* and *changing awareness*. Koss-Chioino identified *relation* as the third core element: Healers expressed and acted on a belief "that a person is continually affected by what other persons are feeling, particularly within families" (Koss-Chioino, 1990, p. 55). In one setting, ritual communications reinforced the client's awareness of this interconnection through reference to individuals as "grains of sand" within the wider universe. Within this study, the centrality of relation is described through the many different ways Tibetan healers referenced interdependence, the client's *relationships* and *tendrel*. The active function of relation as an element of ritual is described here as the ritual of *reconnection with the natural world and community*.

There are some differences in focus: Koss-Chioino's study emphasized the centrality of these elements with reference to the healers' experiences. However, her model suggests that the experiences of spiritual transformation, relation, and empathy are also central to the client's experience, both in traditional healing and within the psychotherapeutic process.

Also, within our research we found three additional core elements to healing: the core rituals of *setting intention*, *mindfulness*, and *creating sacred space.* These rituals prepared the ground for the effectiveness of the ritual elements Koss-Chioino described — spiritual transformation, relation, and radical empathy. More research on the core ritual components of healing across cultures needs to be done in a way that utilizes the combined wisdom of anthropology, psychology, and integrative health so that we can clearly discern whether these elements apply across all cultures, or whether there are functional differences across cultures with regard to their healing paradigms.

# Chapter 14

# Looking Ahead: Creating Cultures of Healing

My intentions, as a researcher, were to explore these traditional Buddhist cultures of healing, with a view towards the ways this may illuminate healing and wellness in contemporary American society. Towards that end, here are a few key findings that have the potential to change the way we practice the healing arts within our wellness centers, psychotherapy offices, and medical centers. These are the healing factors of intention, seeing the connections, mind-body medicine, and the energetic field.

## Intention

First, let's consider the centrality of intention and clear cognition within the healing process. All of the healers referenced the power of intention working in tandem with specific techniques as the catalyst for healing. This intention was supported through the attentional focus of mindfulness. Currently, as Harman and Schlitz (2005) have noted, "consciousness as a causal factor is excluded from the scientific worldview" (p. 367), yet consciousness is central to causality in traditional Buddhist healing and many other integrative modalities. Exploratory studies of intentionality, the relational field of the healer-client interaction, and other consciousness-related factors in healing could benefit from the skills and knowledge within traditional Buddhist healing practices that harness the power of consciousness. The Santa Barbara Institute for Consciousness Studies is currently conducting a five-year compassion and attention longitudinal meditation (CALM) study of the healing effects of meditation, using traditional Tibetan meditation techniques. The study's purposes include the identification of the role that autonomic and inflammatory pathways play in the effect of meditation on stress-responsivity, and the identification of changes in brain functioning that may be associated with meditation-related changes in physiological stress responses (Santa Barbara Institute for Consciousness Studies public announcement, 2013). This study posits that further research could seek convergence between the healer's cultivation of compassion and attention and the client's immune and autonomic response. Research could also be conducted to seek convergence between the client's utilization of meditation and recommended lifestyle changes and the client's immune and autonomic response. In this way, consciousness studies can potentially illuminate the causal factors in illness and wellness.

## Seeing the Connections

A second finding that has ramifications for future research is the centrality of seeing people within relational contexts in Buddhist traditional healing cultures. The paradigm of *paticca samupadda* (interdependence) represents a challenge to Western biomedicine's utilization of mechanistic, linear causality. Rather than seeing cause-and-effect in an isolated material context, this would open the field of the healing sciences to a more multidimensional, systems theory approach — one in line with the new physics. The understanding of self-in-relation expressed by *paticca samupadda* can be seen as compatible with the system-based approaches to the environment, economics, and sociopolitical realities that globalization requires. In fact, as we work towards the development of shared models and practices to resolve public health and environmental crises in our increasingly interconnected world, this way of seeing people-in-relationship could serve as the foundation of a secular ethics of wholeness (Dalai Lama, 2012). A shared ethics of wholeness based on systemic understandings of cause-and-effect could support the development of more healthy, adaptive, and sustainable lifestyles worldwide.

## Healing across Cultures

A related application for our modern world can be found in the correspondences between the core rituals described in this study of Buddhist traditional healers and emergent research on spiritual healing across cultures as represented by the work of Koss-Chioino. Koss-Chioino's compilation, *Spiritual Transformation and Healing*, grew out of the STRP, an interdisciplinary project launched in 2002 to describe the biological, psychosocial, and cultural conditions that support spiritual transformation. Many of the scholars who collaborated on *Spiritual Transformation and Healing* were associated with the STRP. Together they formulated a research agenda that included the questions:

> What is spiritual transformation and is there more than one kind?
> Are there universal elements in the process of spiritual transformation?
> Are the contemporary psychosocial and biosocial models, theories, and methods of study sufficient for these studies and how can they be enlarged to account for the various aspects of spiritual transformation?
> Are specific techniques pathways to spiritual transformation?
> (Katz, 2006)

The scholars' collaborative approach initiated a research focus on spirituality as a medium of healing. In the consideration of the cross-cultural aspects of spirituality as a medium of healing, Koss-Chioino (2006), O'Hara (1997), and other prominent researchers have described relational empathy as a valuable and necessary corrective to the "pervasive bias in Western modernist psychology in favor of objective-materialism" (O'Hara, 1997, p. 12) vis-à-vis the sociocentric, relational knowing that is valued in traditional societies. The Buddhist way of seeing things in connection and relationship could be immensely valuable to clinical psychology, in these particular ways. First, understanding the importance of this way of seeing in traditional healing can help therapists in the construction of culturally hospitable healing spaces for Buddhist clients. Second, these ways of seeing the wholeness within a client could induce Western psychology to be less centered on deficits and diagnoses and more focused on the psychology of human potential. Finally, the relational nature of human wellbeing has implications for the practice of medicine and psychology. When we understand that the body and mind depend upon each other, it makes sense to prescribe psychosocial interventions such as time spent with loved ones to induce physical healing. Conversely, psychotherapy treatment plans may require more diet and exercise interventions.

## Mind-Body Medicine and the Bioenergetic Field

A third potential way these stories transform the field is represented by the reference of a healer to physiocognitive medicine. As we've discussed, Buddhist healing can be understood to work on three levels: body, mind, and subtle energy, which serves as intermediary within the body-mind connection. Through this bidirectional flow of energy and information, consciousness is healed through somatic work, and the body is healed through effecting shifts in awareness. One of the healers referred to the means by which the body-mind shift in awareness takes place as bio-information. The amount of energy conducted through an acupuncture needle, homeopathic treatment, or subtle-energy work is necessarily small, yet it may serve as a signal to the bioenergetic field of the body that catalyzes the body's natural self-organization (Rubik, 2002). The regenerative properties of the bioenergetics field have been supported by clinical evidence conducted in the fields of homeopathy (Voll, 1975), acupuncture (Birch, Itaya, & Manaka, 1995), and reflexology (Rubik, 1995). This insight could be very valuable in developing a new model of the healing process—based on the biofield as a continually dialogical, self-regulating living system that responds dynamically to the energy transmitted by the biofields of the healers and their traditional healing practices. Further research into the emergent properties of the human biofield vis-à-vis complementary medicine is needed.

Ultimately, these directions for future research will require psychologists and life scientists to reconsider certain cherished elements of the Western biomedical model. The experiences of healer co-researchers in this study highlight the centrality of intentionality, attention, relationships, subtle energy, and experiences of numinosity in the creation of health. This absolutely does challenge long-cherished elements of the Western mechanistic worldview. Yet, as medical historian Marc Micozzi (1996) noted:

> When homeopathy or acupuncture is observed to result in a physiologic or clinical response that cannot be explained by the biomedical model, it is not the role of the scientist to deny this reality but rather to modify our explanatory models to account for it. In the end, there is only one reality. (p. 7)

New conceptual frameworks of medicine, based upon living systems studies, would have the potential to integrate biomedical and complementary medical models, utilizing a way of knowing things through their interconnections that is true to the nature of lived experience (Harman & Schlitz, 2005).

## Interpreting Chod: Practice and Research at a Cultural Crossroads

While many of the rituals described here were undertaken by healer-practitioner and client together, or by the client as part of his or her personal development, Chod is explicitly reserved for advanced practitioners. Clients who receive a Chod ritual may be present in a receptive, relaxed state; alternately, the ritual may be done by the Chod practitioner from a distance, with a picture or personal object representing the client. These healers, in addition, described specific Chod rituals that served to prevent hail or alleviate drought. This constitutes a problem for Western researchers of Chod: How, then, does this change of consciousness bring about healing?

Tibetan practitioners explain the effects of Chod ritual through the principle of *tendrel*, a direct experience of the all-pervasive nature of dependent origination.

> One can perceive the world as a logical, rational, sequential, situation. But there is another way of perceiving it, or another way of starting to be, which is where things happen through tendrel, through connection. And they don't have logic. ...That is the space of healing. The space of healing requires that. The purely material world does work on mechanics. Whereas the energy world does not work on mechanics. That's not the ruling principle. The ruling principle is energetics—which are related to connection, and connection has no restriction so far as time or space. It has a connection through meaning. So all of those connections are through meaning. Therefore seemingly miraculous things can happen, because the connection is through meaning—not through time, space or logic. (Lama Jinpa)

Wilhelm's story of the rainmaker, described in Chapter 2, is a close analogy to Chod ritual. The rainmaker, like Tu-Shun, is able to connect with his own wholeness—and through this awakened connection to the "jewel net" of interdependence, the gift of wholeness radiates out through the village, restoring the flow of nature. Within these anecdotes, the depth and the power of the connection of Buddhist causal vision to healing praxis is evident. Through direct or indirect causal relationships with all living things, the work each person does to awaken to his or her innate wholeness anchors that experience of healing for others.

## Transformation of the Author

I was inspired to conduct this study by my own deep commitment to working as a Buddhist teacher and as a healer. In my personal experience as a Buddhist practitioner in Korea and in the United States, the development of my meditation practice included several 90-day retreats. Within the intense physical and psychospiritual rigors of this training, traditional Buddhist healing practices were key to my own progress as a Zen teacher. In part, this project is an expression of gratitude for the professional support and personal friendship of these healers across the lifespan of my meditation practice. Mindful of the effectiveness of these traditional healing practices, I embarked on my own course of study, including MBSR certification and training in energy medicine.

In initiating this research journey it was my intention to integrate my professional life as a Zen teacher and healer with my professional life as a psychology researcher and counselor. It has been exciting to discover the continuing scholarly and praxis-oriented dialogue between these fields, represented by places like the Juniper Foundation, the Menla Center, and the Santa Barbara Institute for Consciousness Studies. Research possibilities related to traditional Buddhist healing now extend beyond the original ground-breaking work of MBSR, to include the fields of Consciousness Studies, Energy Psychology, and Systems Theory. Interdisciplinary work in these fields can create new possibilities for our society in the conceptualization of health and illness; it may support the development of psychospiritual modalities for use in the helping professions that work with the client's body, mind, and energy. On a professional level, this is very exciting.

Through this exploration, I now see these traditional healing practices in their historical context, and fully recognize that the practices of Buddhist meditation and traditional Buddhist healing practices evolved across the centuries together.

It is my sense that this vision of an integrative psychology, one that includes traditional healing practices, has the potential to redress long-standing imbalances in hegemonic power between traditional and modernized cultures. Years ago, my mentor, Elise Boulding, went around the world, studying indigenous cultures and the ways of making peace that were characteristic of each culture. She collected these knowledges and practices in a book, *Creating Cultures of Peace*, that enhanced our society's capacity for peacemaking, and was nominated for the Nobel Peace Prize. In this same vein, it is my intention to actually strengthen our societal capacity for healing by bringing forward the knowledges and practices that are characteristic of Buddhist lineages. By identifying these traditional practices of healing as rituals, it is my intention to draw awareness to the culturally constructed nature of the healing arts. Through the *Story Science* approach, and the use of other practices connected with indigenous research, it has been my intention to model a research approach that itself brings forth tools for multicultural awareness from within the healer, the researcher, and their discourse. The integration of indigenous knowledge with psychology, the bridging of cultures, and the practice of science with reference to the ethics and relational ontology of indigenous ways of knowing, have the potential to bring about more sustainable and integrative ways of living together as a human society. On a personal level, these interviews have confirmed my sense of auspiciousness and benefit through the integration of these diverse ways of knowing. Within each of these interviews, I felt honored by the healers' generosity with their time and energy: Our communities are fortunate to have such healers in their midst. Many of their remarks catalyzed self-reflection and spiritual growth. I felt thankful to serve as a bridge through which their voices are heard within the psychology and healing arts communities. In speaking with clinicians about the study, I have already glimpsed areas of professional psychology practice that will be illuminated by their narratives—particularly, the clinician's use of intentionality, resonance, the creation of sacred space, subtle-energy practices such as Tsa-lung, and spirituality (that is congruent with the client's own meaning-making). It is my intention to continue to facilitate these dialogues between indigenous and modern psychologies through whatever platform becomes available. In my prior studies, clinical psychology had felt disconnected from my spiritual vocation. Through this study, the mind is thoroughly integrated with the heart.

## Buddhist Traditional Healing Praxis: Theoretical and Practical Applications

As discussed in the prior section on future research, it is likely that new ontologies (ways of understanding the nature of reality) and new epistemologies (ways of knowing) will be necessary to understand the effects of traditional healing practices. A careful consideration of the philosophy of science reveals that the ontology of the biosciences was shaped during the Newtonian era, a time period that favored a more atomistic view of reality. This model of reality composed of separate particles then supported an atomistic view of the human condition, and an emphasis upon competitive, individualistic understandings of the self (Barbour, 1990). Now that, through double-slit experiments and other breakthroughs in modern science, every particle is understood to be in relationship with an interdependent whole, the time has come for psychological paradigms that reflect this ontological reality. Buddhist ontologies are congruent with the field of energy psychology and could serve as a potent resource in the formulation of a new paradigm, "science in which consciousness-related phenomena are no longer anomalies but keys to deeper understanding" (Amorok & Schlitz, 2005, p. 374). A shift towards a more engaged and relational scientific ontology would support the development of paradigms of healing that can encompass the empirical reality of integrative medicine practitioners. This ontological shift would then support the development of more philosophically rigorous and experientially accurate research models, so that our ways of doing research are in closer alignment with the nature of reality itself.

There are both theoretical and practical applications for the helping professions in the finding of the therapeutic utility of relational ontology. Client-centered therapy, psychoanalytic self-psychology, and other Western psychotherapeutic modalities have centered upon development through individualization. O'Hara (1997) critiqued the prevalent Western psychological model of a monadic and decontextualized self as culture-bound, inherently egocentric, and a contributing causal factor in modern epidemics of neurosis, depression, self-disorders, and addictive disorders. Within indigenous communities, self-consciousness has been found to be more contextual and holistic (Bourne & Shweder, 1982). The integration of relational ontologies and practices embedded within traditional healing practices may therefore be a valuable and much needed corrective within the Western modernist helping professions. While it can be posited, based on the recent proliferation of mindfulness-related therapies (including MBSR, MBCT (Mindfulness-Based Cognitive Therapy), ACT (Acceptance and Commitment Therapy), DBT (Dialectical Behavioral Therapy), and Hakomi Therapy), as well as other emergent transpersonal modalities, that the movement is already underway, more work needs to be done. The insurance industry's growing emphasis on brief, medical-model therapies and the licensing exam structures that favor cognitive-behavioral approaches define counselors' training, and the field. A more comprehensive integration would tap the deeper potentials of intersubjectivity to support the development of relational, contextual, holistic, and sociocentric skills and knowledges needed to resolve the challenges that face our increasingly diverse and interconnected world.

Another significant contribution of these stories to the field is its in-depth study of cultures of healing. By lifting up these traditional healers' knowledges and practices, new possibilities open up within our society for bringing about both personal and intercultural healing. In order to make this document as accessible as possible to a wide range of communities and cultures, a glossary of terms has been included (see end of book). The medium is the message: through the *Story Science* approach, and the use of other practices connected with indigenous research, it has been my intention to model a research approach that itself brings forth tools for multicultural awareness from within the healer, the scholar, and their conversations.

Finally, a particularly significant contribution of this study to the field is its examination of traditional Buddhist healers' narratives in the context of healing rituals. As previously discussed, discourses on ritual have sometimes been used to objectify the community being studied. However, ritual is simply the collaborative, tangible, and embodied language of meaning-making. Through ritual, we develop relationships, raise consciousness, and develop insight about our world (Wilson, 2008). Mattingly's (2008) study of Western medical performance narratives supported the cultural and psychological reconstruction of Western medical healer-client encounters as healing rituals. These rituals were intrinsic to the healing process; clinical experiences of connection were imbued with relational and spiritual meaning by the patients. The position of these rituals within the mechanistic system of Western medicine, in which they were not consciously recognized or accorded clinical value, resulted in the disruption or neglect of critical aspects of healing (Mattingly, 2008). This study, by shaping transcultural understandings of healing and spirituality, can support the development of new healing paradigms: paradigms that consciously harness the power of ritual to fully engage the power of consciousness in the creation of somatic, psychological, and spiritual health. The current explosion in the fields of psychoneuroimmunology and relational neuroscience research is bringing us closer than ever to a comprehensive understanding of the mind-body connection. Just as biomedical research has discovered new cures for illness through the herbal medicine of the rainforest and traditional Chinese pharmacopeia, modern psychology and the helping professions can also discover new cures in ancient remedies. We are fortunate to live in this transitional time, when this wisdom from the ancient past may illuminate our future. May these practices illuminate our shared path to wholeness.

# Endnotes

1. Kabat-Zinn, J. (2003). Mindfulness-based interventions in context: Past, present, and future. *Clinical Psychology: Science and Practice, 10*(Summer), 144–56; Kabat-Zinn, J. (2005). *Coming to our senses*. New York: Hyperion; Kabat-Zinn, J. (1991). *Full catastrophe living: Using the wisdom of your body and mind to face stress, pain, and illness*. New York: Dell.

2. Benson, H., Beary, J. F., & Carol, M. P. (1974). The relaxation response. *Psychiatry, 37*(1), 37–46.

3. Barbour, I. G. (1990). *Religion in an age of science*. San Francisco: Harper San Francisco.

4. Palmer, P. J., Zajonc, A., & Scribner, M. (2010). *The heart of higher education: A call to renewal*. Hoboken, NJ: John Wiley and Sons.

5. Siegel, D. (2010). *The mindful therapist*. New York: Norton. p. xxii.

6. Bowlby, J. (1969). *Attachment and loss: Vol. 1. Attachment*. New York: Basic Books. p. 194.

7. Badenoch, B. (2008). *Being a brain-wise therapist: A practical guide to interpersonal neurobiology*. New York: Norton.

8. Lewis, T., Amini, F., & Lannon, R. (2000). *A general theory of love*. New York: Random House. p. 62.

9. Lewis, et al. (2000). pp. 70–1, 76.

10. Ainsworth, 1978; Sroufe, A., & Siegel, D. (2011). The verdict is in. *Psychotherapy Networker, 35*(2), 35–9.

11. Studies have shown that an infant whose experience is not mirrored by his mother's expression and behavior recognizes this at a glance, and becomes upset. When there is mutuality in the interaction, the baby is soothed. Lewis, et al. (2000). p. 62.

12. Badenoch, B. (2008). *Being a brain-wise therapist: A practical guide to interpersonal neurobiology*. New York: Norton.

13. Fields, R. D. (2008). Are whales smarter than we are?

*Scientific American, 15.*

14. Siegel, D. (2010). The mindful therapist. New York: Norton. p. 37.

15. Tolstoy, Leo, and Leonard Kent. (2000). *Anna Karenina.* 1st ed. New York: Modern Library, p. 3.

16. Badenoch, B. (2008). *Being a brain-wise therapist: a practical guide to interpersonal neurobiology.* New York: Norton.

17. Sroufe, L. A. (2005). Attachment and development: A prospective, longitudinal study from birth to adulthood. *Attachment & Human Development, 7*(4), 349–67. doi:10.1080/14616730500365928

18. Fonagy, P., Leigh, T., Steele, M., Steele, H., Kennedy, R., Mattoon, G., ... Gerber, A. (1996). The relation of attachment status, psychiatric classification, and response to psychotherapy. *Journal of Consulting and Clinical Psychology, 64*(1), 22–31. doi:10.1037/0022-006x.64.1.22

19. Wolff, M. S., & Ijzendoorn, M. H. (1997). Sensitivity and attachment: A meta-analysis on parental antecedents of infant attachment. *Child Development, 68*(4), 571. doi:10.2307/1132107

20. Puig, J., Englund, M. M., Simpson, J. A., & Collins, W. A. (2013). Predicting adult physical illness from infant attachment: A prospective longitudinal study. *Health Psychology, 32*(4), 409–17. doi:10.1037/a0028889

21. Felitti, V. J., Anda, R. F., Nordenberg, D., Williamson, D. F., Spitz, A. M., Edwards, V., ... Marks, J. S. (1998). Relationship of childhood abuse and household dysfunction to many of the leading causes of death in adults. *American Journal of Preventive Medicine, 14*(4), 245–58. doi:10.1016/s0749-3797(98)00017-8.

22. Lazar, S. W., Kerr, C. E., Wasserman, R. H., Gray, J. R., Greve, D. N., Treadway, M. T., . . . Fischl, B. (2005). Meditation experience is associated with increased cortical thickness. *NeuroReport, 16*(17), 1893–7. doi:10.1097/01.

wnr.0000186598.66243.19

23. Hanson, R. (2009). *Buddha's brain: The practical neuroscience of happiness, love, and wisdom.* Oakland, CA: New Harbinger Publications.

# Acknowledgements

I owe a debt of gratitude to many people—all those in the US, in Korea and Nepal whose insight and help made this book possible.

First, I would like to thank all my co-researchers for their generosity in time, insight and energy, without whom this book could not have been written.

Special gratitude is due to Dr. Eduardo Duran, Lama Tsering Ngodup, Lama John Makransky, Tenzin Wangyal Rinpoche, and Geshe Chaphur for sharing their profound wisdom which was essential to my understanding of Buddhist practice and research.

I thank my dissertation advisor, Dr. Nancy Rowe, for her insight and for helping me to attend to all levels of the writing process, craftsmanship and content. Thank you as well to my committee members, Dr. Ann Drake and Dr. Tina Amorok, for their great insight, energy and care.

I thank Dr. Gabriela Mihalache for her gracious counsel and mentorship, and her accessibility throughout the process of doctoral research and writing.

Thank you to all my sanghas (meditation communities) which have been wellsprings of presence and renewal during this process: Wellesley Buddhist Community, Empty Gate Zen Center, Dharma Zen Center, Gyalshen Institute, North County Zen Circle and Four Vows Sangha.

Thank you to Jose Shinzan Palma, Kate Lila Wheeler and John Kotatsu Bailes, for the immeasurable gifts of your Dharma friendship.

Thank you to the CIHS / Encinitas Healing Circle for the gifts of spiritual friendship and community.

Thank you as well to Omega Institute—in particular, its seasonal staff who have provided a spiritual home across fifteen summers of writing. Their service is compassion in action.

Thank you also to Brett Bevell for your support and insight over many years.

Many people have provided personal support—in particular I would like to extend gratitude to medical Qi Gong teacher Robert Peng, Qi Gong practitioner Eugene Vodovov, Shiatsu practitioner Gi Pamperien, acupuncturists Patrick Cunningham and Dody Chang, herbalist Tommy Priester and the integrative osteopath Steven Weiss who have brought me to wholeness of body, mind and spirit.

Finally, I thank my family for their care and patience. I am so grateful to them for supporting this work.

While acknowledging the support I have received from all those mentioned (and many unnamed), I bear sole responsibility for any shortcomings manifested in this work.

# Permissions

### *Eight Cases of Basic Goodness not to be Shunned*

Composed by the lord Götsangpa. Under the guidance of Khenpo Tsultrim Gyamtso Rinpoche, translated and arranged by Jim Scott, Karme Choling, Barnet, Vermont, August 1997. Translation copyright 2012, Jim Scott. For further teachings on this topic, please also see www.ktgrinpoche.org and ktgr. dscloud.me/moodle

# References

Abram, D. (1996). *The spell of the sensuous.* New York, NY: Pantheon Books.

Amorok, T., & Schlitz, M. (2005). Honoring multiple ways of knowing. In T. Amorok, M. Marcozzi, & M. Schlitz (Eds.), *Consciousness and healing: Integral approaches to mind-body medicine* (pp. 355–61). St. Louis, MO: Elsevier.

Arai, P. (2013). *Bringing Zen home: The healing heart of Japanese women's rituals.* Honolulu, HI: University of Hawaii Press.

Armstrong, K. (2004). *Buddha.* New York, NY: Penguin.

Atkinson, M., McCraty, R., Tiller, W. A., & Tomasino, D. (1998). The electricity of touch: Detection and measurement of cardiac energy exchange between people. In K. H. Pribram (Ed.), *Brain and values: Is a biological science of values possible?* (pp. 359–79). Mahwah, NJ: Lawrence Erlbaum Associates.

Badenoch, B. (2008). *Being a brain-wise therapist.* New York, NY: Norton.

Barbour, I. G. (1990). *Religion in an age of science.* San Francisco, CA: Harper San Francisco.

Benson, H. (1991). Mind/body interactions including Tibetan studies. In Dalai Lama, D. Goleman, & R. A. Thurman (Eds.), *Mindscience: An East-West dialogue* (pp. 37–50). Boston, MA: Wisdom.

Benson, H., Beary, J. F., & Carol, M. P. (1974). The relaxation response. *Psychiatry, 37*(1), 37–46.

Berzin, A. (2000). Introductory comparison of the five Tibetan traditions of Buddhism and Bon.
*The Berzin archives.* Retrieved from http://www.berzinar chives.com/web/en/archives/study/comparison_budd hist_traditions/tibetan_traditions/intro_compar_5_ traditions_buddhism_bon.html

Beyer, Stephen. (1977). Notes on the vision quest in early Mahāyāna. In Lewis Lancaster (Ed.), *Prajñāpāramitā and*

*Related Systems* (pp. 329–40). Berkeley, CA: Berkeley Buddhist Studies Series.

Birch, S., Itaya, K., & Manaka, Y. (1995). *Chasing the dragon's tail: The theory and practice of acupuncture in the work of Yoshio Manaka*. Brookline, MA: Paradigm.

Birnbaum, R. (1979). *The healing Buddha*. Boston, MA: Shambhala.

Blofield, J. (1977). *Mantras: Sacred words of power*. New York, NY: E. P. Dutton.

Bodhi, B. (1998). Message. In S. Thera (Ed.), *The way of mindfulness: The Satipatthana Sutta and its commentary*. Retrieved from http://www.accesstoinsight.org/lib/authors/soma/wayof. html#msg

Bodhi, B. (Trans.). (2000). *The connected discourses of the Buddha: A translation of the Samyutta Nikaya*. Boston, MA: Wisdom.

Bohm, D. (2002). *Wholeness and the implicate order*. London, UK: Routledge and Kegan Paul.

Bourne, E. J., & Shweder, R. A. (1982). Does the concept of the person vary cross-culturally? In R. A. LeVine & R. A. Shweder (Eds.), *Culture theory: Essays on mind, self, and emotion* (pp. 97–137). Rotterdam, Netherlands: Springer.

Bowlby, J. 1969. *Attachment and loss: Vol. 1. Attachment*. New York, NY: Basic Books.

Braud, W., & Schlitz, M. (1997). Distant intentionality and healing: Assessing the evidence. *Alternative Therapies in Health and Medicine, 3*(6), 62–73.

Brown, A. (2013). Everyday Chod—Practicing Chod. *Everyday Chod*. Retrieved from http://everydaychod.com/articles/ practicingChod.shtml

Cabezon, J. I. (2009). *Tibetan ritual*. Oxford, UK: Oxford University Press.

Carpenter, J. E., & Rhys Davids, T. W. (Trans.). (1977). *Digha Nikaya: The dialogues of the Buddha*. London, UK: Routledge and Kegan Paul.

Chaoul, A. (2011). Re-integrating the dharmic perspective in biobehavioural research of a "Tibetan Yoga" (tsalung trülkhor) intervention for people with cancer. *Medicine Between Science and Religion: Explorations on Tibetan Grounds, 10,* 297.

Chaoul-Reich, A., Cohen, L., Fouladi, R. T., Rodriguez, M., & Warneke, C. (2004). Psychological adjustment and sleep quality in a randomized trial of the effects of a Tibetan yoga intervention in patients with lymphoma. *Cancer, 100*(10), 2253–60. doi:10.1002/cncr.20236

Chenagtsang, N. (2014, March 6). *The Yuthok Nyingthig spiritual tradition.* Lecture conducted at the Sorig Institute, Oakland, CA.

Chozen-Bays, J., Levy, M., Rhodes, B., & Shlim, D. (2005). Ultimately, you're healthy; relatively, you die. *Shambhala Sun, 13*(5), 36–41, 87–8.

Cleary, T. (Trans.). (1993). *The flower ornament sutra.* Boston, MA: Shambhala.

Cleary, T. (Trans.). (2000). The jewel net of Indra. In S. Kaza & K. Kraft (Eds.), *Dharma rain: Sources of Buddhist environmentalism* (pp. 58–60). Boston, MA: Shambhala.

Clifford, T. (2006*). Tibetan Buddhist medicine and psychiatry.* Delhi, India: Motilal Banarsidass.

Cupchik, J. W. (2013). The Tibetan gCod Ḍamaru—A reprise: Symbolism, function, and difference in a Tibetan adept's interpretive community. *Asian Music, 44*(1), 113–39.

Dakpa, T., & Dodson-Lavelle, B. (2009). "Subtle" psychosomatic aspects of Tibetan medicine. *Annals of the New York Academy of Sciences, 1172,* 181–5. doi:10.1196/annals.1393.015

Dalai Lama. (1991). The Buddhist concept of mind. In Dalai Lama, D. Goleman, & R. A. Thurman (Eds.), *Mindscience: An East-West dialogue* (pp. 11–18). Boston, MA: Wisdom.

Dalai Lama. (2012). *Beyond religion: Ethics for a whole world.* New York, NY: Random House.

Duran, E. (2014). Story science. In R. Goodman & P. Gorski (Eds.), *Decolonizing "multicultural" counseling and psychology: Visions for social justice theory and practice* (pp. 22–37). New

York, NY: Springer.

Ehlers, E., & Gethmann, C. (2010). *Environment across cultures*. New York, NY: Springer.

Eisenstein, C. (n.d.). Every Act a Ceremony. Retrieved June 30, 2019, from https://charleseisenstein.org/essays/ceremony/

Felitti, V. J., Anda, R. F., Nordenberg, D., Williamson, D. F., Spitz, A. M., Edwards, V., ... Marks, J. S. (1998). Relationship of childhood abuse and household dysfunction to many of the leading causes of death in adults. *American Journal of Preventive Medicine, 14*(4), 245–58. doi:10.1016/s0749-3797(98)00017-8

Fields, R. D. 2008. Are whales smarter than we are? *Scientific American, 15*.

Fine, M. (1994). Working the hyphens: Reinventing self and other in qualitative research. In N. Denzin & Y. Lincoln (Eds.), *Handbook of qualitative research* (pp. 70–82). Thousand Oaks, CA: Sage.

Fonagy, P., Leigh, T., Steele, M., Steele, H., Kennedy, R., Mattoon, G., ... Gerber, A. (1996). The relation of attachment status, psychiatric classification, and response to psychotherapy. *Journal of Consulting and Clinical Psychology, 64*(1), 22–31. doi:10.1037/0022-006x.64.1.22

Ghosananda, M. (1991). *Step by step*. Berkeley, CA: Parallax.

Gotsangpa, G., & Scott, J. (Trans.). (2012). *Eight Cases of Basic Goodness not to be Shunned*. Barnet, VT: Marpa Translation Committee.

Hannah, B. (1991). *Jung, his life and work: A biographical memoir*. Boston, MA: Shambhala.

Hanson, R. 2009. Buddha's brain: The practical neuroscience of happiness, love, and wisdom. Oakland, CA: New Harbinger Publications.

Hardy, J. (2014, January 1). Sacred space. *Patheos Library*. Retrieved from http://www.patheos.com/Library/Buddhism/Ritual-Worship-Devotion-Symbolism/Sacred-Space.html

Harman, W., & Schlitz, M. (2005). The implications of alternative and complementary medicine for science and the scientific process. In T. Amorok, M. Marcozzi, & M. Schlitz (Eds.), *Consciousness and healing: Integral approaches to mind-body medicine* (pp. 361–76). St. Louis, MO: Elsevier.

Johnson, W., Robinson, R., & Bhikkhu, T. (2005). *Buddhist religion: A historical introduction*. Beverly, MA: Wadsworth.

Kabat-Zinn, J. (1991). *Full catastrophe living: Using the wisdom of your body and mind to face stress, pain, and illness*. New York, NY: Dell.

Kabat-Zinn, J. (2003). Mindfulness-based interventions in context: Past, present, and future. *Clinical Psychology: Science and Practice, 10*(Summer), 144–56.

Kabat-Zinn, J. (2005). *Coming to our senses*. New York, NY: Hyperion.

Kaptchuk, T. (1999). *The web that has no weaver: Understanding Chinese medicine*. Chicago, IL: Contemporary Books.

Katz, S. (2004). *The Spiritual Transformation Scientific Research Program*. Philadelphia, PA: Metanexus Institute on Religion and Science.

Katz, S. (2006). Foreword. In J. D. Koss-Chioino & P. J. Hefner (Eds.), *Spiritual transformation and healing: Anthropological, theological, neuroscientific, and clinical perspectives* (pp. ix–xii). Oxford, UK: Rowman Altamira.

Koss-Chioino, J. D. (2006a). Spiritual transformation, relation and radical empathy: Core components of the ritual healing process. *Transcultural Psychiatry, 43*(4), 652–70.

Koss-Chioino, J. D. (2006b). Spiritual transformation and radical empathy in ritual healing and therapeutic relationships. In J. Koss-Chioino & P. J. Hefner (Eds.), *Spiritual transformation and healing: Anthropological, theological, neuroscientific, and clinical perspectives* (pp. 45–61). Oxford, UK: Rowman Altamira.

Kressing, F. (2011). Shamanism as medical prevention? A case study from Ladakh, Northwest-India. *Medizin, Gesellschaft, und Geschichte: Jahrbuch des Instituts für Geschichte der Medizin der Robert Bosch Stiftung, 30,* 229.

Kvaerne, P., & Thargyal, R. (1993). *Bon, Buddhism and democracy: The building of a Tibetan national identity.* Copenhagen, Denmark: Nordic Institute of Asian Studies.

Lad, V. (2002). *Textbook of Ayurveda fundamental principles.* Albuquerque, NM: Ayurvedic Press.

Lazar, S. W., Bush, G., Gollub, R. L., Fricchione, G. L., Khalsa, G., & Benson, H. (2000). Functional brain mapping of the relaxation response and meditation. NeuroReport, 7(11), 1581–5.

Lewis, T., Amini, F., & Lannon, R. (2000). *A general theory of love.* New York, NY: Random House.

Macy, J. R. (1978). *Interdependence: Mutual causality in early Buddhist teachings and general systems theory* (Doctoral Dissertation). Available from ProQuest Dissertations and Theses. (UMI No. 7908553)

Makransky, J. (2000). Historical consciousness as an offering to the trans-historical Buddha. In J. Makransky & R. Jackson (Eds.), *Buddhist theology: Critical reflections by contemporary Buddhist scholars* (pp. 111–35). New York, NY: Routledge.

Mattingly, C. (2004). Performance narratives in the clinical world. In B. Hurwitz, T. Greenhalgh, & V. Skultans (Eds.), *Narrative research in health and illness* (pp. 73–94). Malden, MA: BMJ Books.

Metanexus Institute on Religion and Science. (2004). *Spiritual Transformation Scientific Research Program prospectus.* New York, NY: Metanexus Institute.

Micozzi, M. S. (1996). Characteristics of complementary and alternative medicine. In M. Micozzi (Ed.), *Fundamentals of complementary and alternative medicine* (pp. 3–8). New York, NY: Churchill Livingstone.

Nalanda Translation Committee. (2003). *Dependent arising/tendrel.* Retrieved from http://nalandatranslation.org/offerings/choosing-the-right-word/dependent-arising-tendrel/

Ninivaggi, F. J. (2008). *Ayurveda: A comprehensive guide to traditional Indian medicine for the West*. Westport, CT: Praeger.

Novick, R. (1999). *Fundamentals of Tibetan Buddhism*. Freedom, CA: Crossing Press.

O'Hara, M. (1997). Relational empathy: Beyond modernist egocentricism to postmodern holistic contextualism. In A. C. Bohart & L. S. Greenberg (Eds.), *Empathy reconsidered: New directions in psychotherapy* (pp. 295–319). Washington, DC: American Psychological Association. doi:10.1037/10226-013

Peters, Larry. (2016). *Tibetan shamanism: Ecstasy and healing*. Berkeley, CA: North Atlantic.

Phabongkha bde chen snying-po. (1984). *Chod: Cutting off the truly existent "I"* (Lama Thupten Zopa Rinpoche, Ed. & Trans.). London, UK: Wisdom.

Preece, R. (2006). *The psychology of Buddhist tantra*. Boston, MA: Snow Lion.

Puig, J., Englund, M. M., Simpson, J. A., & Collins, W. A. (2013). Predicting adult physical illness from infant attachment: A prospective longitudinal study. *Health Psychology, 32*(4), 409–17. doi:10.1037/a0028889

Ramanan, K. V. (1987). *Nāgārjuna's philosophy as presented in the Maha-prajñāpāramitā-śstra* (Vol. 6). New Delhi, India: Motilal Banarsidass.

Ray, R. (2008). *Touching enlightenment: Finding realization in the body*. Boulder, CO: Sounds True.

Rinpoche, S. (1992). *The Tibetan book of living and dying*. New York, NY: HarperCollins.

Rinpoche, T. (2006). 2. The first three preliminary practices. Retrieved June 29, 2019, from http://www.rinpoche.com/teachings/chod.htm

Rinpoche, T. W. (2004). Interview. In H. Webb (Ed.), *Traveling between the worlds: Conversations with contemporary shamans* (pp. 230–8). Charlottesville, VA: Hampton Roads.

Rinpoche, T. W. (2011). *Awakening the sacred body* (M. Vaughn,

Ed.). New York, NY: Hay House.

Rinpoche, T. W., & Wangyal, T. (2002). *Healing with form, energy and light: The five elements in Tibetan shamanism, tantra, and dzogchen.* Boston, MA: Snow Lion.

Rubik, B. (1995). Can Western science provide a foundation for acupuncture? *Alternative therapies in health and medicine, 1*(4), 41–7.

Rubik, B. (2002). The biofield hypothesis: Its biophysical basis and role in medicine. *The Journal of Alternative & Complementary Medicine, 8*(6), 703–17.

Samuel, G. (2014). Body and mind in Tibetan medicine and tantric Buddhism. In T. Hofer (Ed.), *Bodies in balance: The art of Tibetan Medicine (pp. 32–45).* New York, NY: Rubin Museum of Art.

Schlitz, M. (2005). The integral impulse: An emerging model for health and healing. In T. Amorok, M. Marcozzi, & M. Schlitz (Eds.), *Consciousness and healing: Integral approaches to mind-body medicine* (pp. xxxviii–xlv). St. Louis, MO: Elsevier.

Schuhmacher, S., & Woerner, G. (1991). *Shambhala dictionary of Buddhism and Zen.* Boston, MA: Shambhala.

Siegel, D. (2007). *The mindful brain.* New York, NY: Norton.

Siegel, D. (2010a). *Mindsight.* New York, NY: Bantam.

Siegel, D. (2010b). *The mindful therapist.* New York, NY: Norton.

Sifers, S., & Documentary Educational Resources. (2007). *Fate of the lhapa.* Watertown, MA: Documentary Educational Resources.

Snyder, G. (2000). Nets of beads, webs of cells. In S. Kaza & K. Kraft (Eds.), *Dharma rain: Sources of Buddhist environmentalism* (pp. 346–52). Boston, MA: Shambhala.

Sroufe, A., & Siegel, D. (2011). The verdict is in. *Psychotherapy Networker, 35*(2), 35–9.

Sroufe, L. A. (2005). Attachment and development: A prospective, longitudinal study from birth to adulthood. *Attachment & Human Development, 7*(4), 349–67.

Subramanian, M. (2002). *Travels of possessed women on the*

*brink of memory: Embodied faith, nostalgia and fear in modern Japan* (Doctoral Dissertation). Available from ProQuest Dissertations and Theses. (UMI No. 3048627)

Subramanian, M. (2012, January). *Journey to heal across cultures.* Keynote lecture given at Global PhD Seminar, Institute for Transpersonal Psychology, Los Gatos, CA.

Sumegi, A. (2008). *Dreamworlds of shamanism and Tibetan Buddhism: The third place.* Albany, NY: SUNY Press.

Tatz, M. (Trans.). (1985). *Buddhism and healing: Demieville's article "Byo" from Hobogirin.* New York, NY: University Press of America.

Thanh, M. (2001). *Sutra of the Medicine Buddha* (P. D. Leigh, Trans.). North Hills, CA: International Buddhist Monastic Institute. Retrieved from http://www.buddhanet.net/pdf_ file/medbudsutra.pdf

Thera, N. (Trans.). (2011). The foundations of mindfulness: Satipatthana Sutra. *Access to Insight, 7*(June 2010). Retrieved from http://www.accesstoinsight.org/lib/authors/nyanasatta/ wheel019.html

Thondup, T. (2013). *Boundless healing: Meditation exercises to enlighten the mind and heal the body.* Boston, MA: Shambhala.

Thurman, R. (Trans.). (1991). *The holy teaching of Vimalakirti.* Delhi, India: Motilal Banarsidass.

Tolstoy, Leo, and Leonard Kent. (2000). *Anna Karenina.* 1st ed. New York, NY: Modern Library, p. 3.

Trungpa, C. (2003). *Glimpses of realization: The three bodies of enlightenment* (J. Lief, Ed.). Halifax, Nova Scotia, Canada: Vajradhatu.

Trungpa, C. (2007). *Shambhala: The sacred path of the warrior.* Boston, MA: Shambhala.

Tsiknopoulos, E. (Trans.) (2019). *Field of blessing. Translated from the Tibetan for this book.*

Vargas, I. (2003). *Falling to pieces, emerging whole: Suffering illness and healing renunciation in the life of Gelongma Palmo* (Doctoral

Dissertation). Available from ProQuest Dissertations and Theses. (UMI No. 3091747)

Van der Kolk, B. (2015). *The body keeps the score: Brain, mind, and body in the healing of trauma.* New York, NY: Penguin Books.

Voll, R. (1975). Twenty years of electroacupuncture diagnosis in Germany. A progress report. *American Journal of Acupuncture, 3(1),* 7–17.

Wilber, K. (2000). *Integral psychology: Consciousness, spirit, psychology, therapy.* Boston, MA: Shambhala.

Wilson, S. (2008). *Research is ceremony.* Halifax, Nova Scotia, Canada: Fernwood Publishing.

Wolff, M. S., & Ijzendoorn, M. H. (1997). Sensitivity and attachment: A meta-analysis on parental antecedents of infant attachment. *Child Development, 68*(4), 571. doi:10.2307/1132107

# Glossary of Terms

## Buddhist Terms

**Avalokitesvara:** Sanskrit name for the Bodhisattva of compassion. Chinese: *Kuan Yin*. Korean: *Kwan Seum Bosal*.

**Ayurvedic healing:** an ancient system of traditional healing that originated in India, in the context of Buddhist, Jain, and Hindu schools of thought.

**Bodhicitta:** awakened heart-mind.

**Bodhisattva:** an archetype of compassion. Traditionally described as an awakened being who stays in the world, rather than transcending it, in order to relieve suffering and benefit all beings. Alt: someone who has the compassionate direction to be of service.

**Bon tradition (or, Bonpo):** an ancient indigenous spiritual tradition of Tibet which preceded Buddhism, and was then influenced by Buddhism. Considered one of Tibet's five spiritual traditions.

**Buddha:** awakened one. Refers to the historical Shakyamuni Buddha, Siddharta Gautama; to the awakened beings who have come before and after, and to the original nature we all possess which is clear, compassionate, and wise.

**Chod:** a Tibetan ritual which harnesses the power of fear to bring about liberation. Chod ritual includes *phowa* and *tonglen* practices.

**Conduct of equal taste:** in Vajrayana Buddhism, the practice of using all phenomena, thoughts, and perceptions as the path to awakening.

**Creating space:** making a space sacred through ritual. All ritual activities in Buddhism can be considered to evoke sacred energies, and thus create a sacred space (a space identified as a manifestation of the sacred).

**Dakini:** in Buddhism, a feminine principle that serves as a protector of the teachings; may also be a feminine wisdom being who transmits the teaching. Associated with the element of space, the quality of emptiness, primordial energy, and sky-like mind.

**Dependent origination:** also referred to as interdependent origination, mutual causality, mutual arising, and paticca samupadda. See *Paticca samupadda*

**Dharma:** truth, the nature of things, phenomena. Refers to the teaching of the Buddha, as this reflects natural law.

**Dharmakaya:** one of the three "bodies" of reality (*trikaya*); specifically, the one representing the body of pure enlightenment, or universal energy.

**Dzogchen:** a body of teachings within Tibetan Buddhism that aim at actualizing the natural state of wisdom and clear compassion.

**Embodied presence:** "To be awake, to be enlightened, is to be fully and completely embodied. To be fully embodied means to be at one with who we are, in every respect, including our physical being, our emotions and the totality of our karmic situation. It is to be entirely present to who we are and to the journey of our own becoming" (Ray, 2008 p. vii).

**Explicate order:** in the work of David Bohm, the dimension of all tangible forms.

**Form and Emptiness:** in Buddhism, *form* refers to the tangible shapes energy takes in the world, to bring about all phenomena: the physical world and explicit ways of knowing. *Emptiness* refers to that energy that underlies all things, out of which everything arises and to which everything returns; it is connected with tacit ways of knowing. The interplay of form and emptiness is witnessed through the ephemeral nature of all phenomena, which come and go like waves upon the ocean.

**Implicate order:** in the work of David Bohm, that dimension of Truth and energy which serves as the matrix of all tangible forms.

**Klesha:** (Sanskrit) a negative mental state.

**Lineage:** in Buddhism, a line of transmission of teachings, from teacher to student, which traces back to Shakyamuni Buddha.

**Mahayana:** a branch of Buddhism which emphasizes the attainment of enlightenment for the benefit of all sentient beings, through compassionate action.

**Mandala:** within Tibetan Buddhism, a template of perfected being which symbolizes the inner world and the macrocosm.

**Manjushri:** in Mahayana Buddhism, the archetype of nondual wisdom.

**Mantra:** a phrase that is repeated as a meditative practice to bring the mind to a state of concentration. Mantras may have specialized uses, e.g. to bring healing, or to connect with elemental energy. However, their central purpose is always to awaken the practitioner's heart/mind (Blofield, 1977).

**Maya:** (Sanskrit) the play of phenomena, within constant change, upon the pure energy of nonduality, which can be envisioned as waves upon an infinite ocean.

**Moxibustion:** the therapeutic burning of the herb mugwort in traditional medicine.

**Nagarjuna:** a renowned second-century CE Buddhist teacher and philosopher who served as head of Nalanda University, and is credited with expounding the Mahayana Buddhist concept of *sunyata* (emptiness). Nagarjuna was also an Ayurvedic healer.

**Nama rupa:** (Sanskrit) "name and form." The physical and psychological processes which constitute a human being.

**Nirmanakaya:** one of the three "bodies" of reality (*trikaya*); specifically, the one representing the body that is physically manifest, and lives within time and space.

**Paticca samupadda:** the teaching that each element of existence is conditioned by other elements. Associated with Buddha's original insight at the moment of Enlightenment.

**Phowa practice:** the Tibetan practice of preparing to attain the highest level of awareness while transitioning through death.

**Prajna Paramita:** (Sanskrit) perfection of wisdom: one of the six paramitas (perfections) which are considered positive states which one should cultivate in order to awaken. Also commonly refers to the Prajna Paramita Sutra, which describes the Buddhist teaching of nonduality.

**Sambhogakaya:** one of the three "bodies" of reality (*trikaya*); specifically, the one representing the body that mediates between the pure enlightenment/energy of Dharmakaya and the tangible form of Nirmanakaya.

**Samskara:** (Sanskrit) memory trace which surfaces in conscious awareness.

**Sangha:** community. Refers to the original assembly of monks and nuns, to Buddhist temple and meditation center communities, and to all beings, since all beings are ultimately part of our family.

**Sowa Rigpa:** literally understood, refers to Tibetan medicine. Can also be translated as "healing science," or the "nourishment of awareness."

**Sunyata:** (Sanskrit) emptiness. In Mahayana Buddhism, the teaching that all things are empty of an essential nature.

**Sutra:** traditionally refers to a record of the teaching of the historical Buddha, or another highly revered ancestral Buddhist teacher.

**Tattvas:** subelements that exist within the traditional five elements.

**Tendrel:** auspicious connections, auspicious coincidence based on the interplay of cause-and-effect, whether visible or unseen. Comes from the teaching on *pratitya-samutpada*, the law of cause and effect.

**Therapeutic attunement:** therapists' capacity to "focus our attention on others and take their essence into our own inner world" (Siegel, 2010, p. 34).

**Theravadan Buddhism:** a branch of Buddhism which emphasizes assiduous adherence to the historical teachings and practices of the Buddha, and the transcendence of the cycle of life and death through the attainment of insight.

**Tonglen:** "a meditation practice in which the practitioner actively chooses to take on the sufferings of others" (Novick, 1999, p. 180).

**Trikaya:** in Mahayana Buddhism, the three "bodies" of reality, and the three "bodies" of the Buddha, a model that describes the presence of the transcendent within the immanent.

**Unintegration:** a psychological state, first identified by Donald Winicott, that is characterized as being rather than doing, which has parallels in Buddhist experience.

**Upaya:** (Sanskrit) skillful means. A Mahayana Buddhist concept which "includes the infinite scope of activities and methods through which buddhas and bodhisattvas communicate Dharma (the Buddhist teaching) in the precise ways appropriate to the capacities of all living beings" (Makransky, 2000, pp. 116–17).

**Vajrasattva:** the Tibetan Buddhist Bodhisattva whose aspect of Buddha nature is that of purification. He is visualized as pure white, seated in lotus posture, holding a vajra and a bell.

**Yidam:** in Tibetan Buddhism, a deity considered to be an emanation of enlightened mind.

## Neurobiology Terms

**Amygdala:** a small, almond-shaped region of the brain which is part of the limbic system and affects fear responses, memory, and emotional learning.

**Brainstem:** the lower region of the brain, which links with the spinal cord, conducting energy and information between the brain and the body. It integrates body-brain functions, and thus regulates the cardiovascular system, the respiratory system, sensitivity, awareness, and consciousness.

**Hippocampus:** a region of the brain which is part of the limbic system. Its functions include memory and spatial awareness.

**Insula cortex:** a part of the brain situated deep in the sulcus between the temporal lobe and the frontal lobe which affects emotion. Its functions include perception, motor control, self-awareness, cognitive function, and interpersonal experience.

**Limbic system:** the interconnected structures in the brain that support emotion, behaviour, and memory functions; a significant part of the body-mind feedback loop.

**Neocortex:** the newest part of the brain to evolve; functions include thought and language, spatial reasoning, sensory perception, and motor commands. Includes the prefrontal cortex.

**Neurotransmitter:** a chemical that transmits signals from a neuron to a target cell across a synapse (gap). Many of these affect our arousal level and emotions.

**Prefrontal cortex:** an area in the front of the brain which is associated with higher functions such as insight, attunement, emotional effective balance, fear modulation, empathy, ethics, and intuition.

MANTRA
BOOKS

## EASTERN RELIGION & PHILOSOPHY

We publish books on Eastern religions and philosophies. Books
that aim to inform and explore the various traditions that began in
the East and have migrated West.
If you have enjoyed this book, why not tell other readers by
posting a review on your preferred book site.

# Recent bestsellers from MANTRA BOOKS are:

## The Way Things Are
A Living Approach to Buddhism
Lama Ole Nydahl
An introduction to the teachings of the Buddha, and how to make
use of these teachings in everyday life.
Paperback: 978-1-84694-042-2 ebook: 978-1-78099-845-9

## Back to the Truth
5000 Years of Advaita
Dennis Waite
A demystifying guide to Advaita for both those new to, and those
familiar with this ancient, non-dualist philosophy from India.
Paperback: 978-1-90504-761-1 ebook: 978-184694-624-0

## Shinto: A Celebration of Life
Aidan Rankin
Introducing a gentle but powerful spiritual pathway reconnecting
humanity with Great Nature and affirming all aspects of life.
Paperback: 978-1-84694-438-3 ebook: 978-1-84694-738-4

## In the Light of Meditation
Mike George
A comprehensive introduction to the practice of meditation and
the spiritual principles behind it. A 10 lesson meditation
programme with CD and internet support.
Paperback: 978-1-90381-661-5

## The Less Dust the More Trust
Participating in The Shamatha Project, Meditation and Science
Adeline van Waning, MD PhD
The inside-story of a woman participating in frontline meditation
research, exploring the interfaces of mind-practice, science and
psychology.
Paperback: 978-1-78099-948-7 ebook: 978-1-78279-657-2


## I Know How To Live, I Know How To Die
The Teachings of Dadi Janki: A warm, radical, and life-affirming
view of who we are, where we come from, and what time is calling
us to do
Neville Hodgkinson
Life and death are explored in the context of frontier science and
deep soul awareness.
Paperback: 978-1-78535-013-9 ebook: 978-1-78535-014-6


## Living Jainism
An Ethical Science
Aidan Rankin, Kanti V. Mardia
A radical new perspective on science rooted in intuitive awareness
and deductive reasoning.
Paperback: 978-1-78099-912-8 ebook: 978-1-78099-911-1


## A Path of Joy
Popping into Freedom
Paramananda Ishaya
A simple and joyful path to spiritual enlightenment.
Paperback: 978-1-78279-323-6 ebook: 978-1-78279-322-9